# THIS IS MY CENTURY

For my people lending their strength to the years,
to the gone years and the now years and the maybe years, . . .

# THIS IS MY CENTURY

## NEW AND COLLECTED POEMS

### MARGARET WALKER

THE UNIVERSITY OF GEORGIA PRESS
ATHENS AND LONDON

Designed by Sandra Strother Hudson
Set in Fairfield and Gill Sans types
The paper in this book meets the guidelines
for permanence and durability of the Committee on
Production Guidelines for Book Longevity of the
Council on Library Resources.

Printed in the United States of America

93   92   91   90   89     5   4   3   2   1

Library of Congress Cataloging in Publication Data

Walker, Margaret, 1915–
   This is my century : new and collected poems /
Margaret Walker.
      p. cm.
   Bibliography: p.
   ISBN 0-8203-1134-0 (alk. paper). — ISBN
0-8203-1135-9 (pbk.: alk. paper)
   I. Title.
PS3545.A517T47 1989                                     88-8016
811'.54—dc19                                                CIP

British Library Cataloging in Publication Data available

This volume contains three previously published
collections of poems by Margaret Walker:
*For My People.* New Haven: Yale University Press, 1942.
*Prophets for a New Day.* Detroit: Broadside Press, 1970.
*October Journey.* Detroit: Broadside Press, 1973.

Frontispiece: *For My People—With Love, for Margaret,
My Friend,* silk screen by Elizabeth Catlett, 1987
(Printed at the Arizona State University Visual Arts
Research Institute. Words from "For My People," by
Margaret Walker. Used by permission.)

# CONTENTS

## FOR MY PEOPLE

*These poems did not appear in the original edition of *For My People*, but
were published in 1938 in *Opportunity, A Journal of Negro Life*.

## PROPHETS FOR A NEW DAY

## OCTOBER JOURNEY

## THIS IS MY CENTURY

## FARISH STREET

# PREFACE

If I could write my epitaph it would read:

Here lies Margaret Walker
    Poet and Dreamer

She tried to make her life
    a Poem.

The five volumes of poetry collected in this edition contain a record of more than fifty years of my life as a poet. They represent one hundred of my best poems selected from a possible thousand. I wrote my early poems when I was eleven or twelve, thirteen or fourteen years old, while I was in high school at Gilbert Academy in New Orleans. My father told my mother that my writing was only a puberty urge and not the mark of a genius. Nevertheless, it was my father who gave me a datebook as a Christmas present when I was only twelve and a half years old. He said I should keep all my poems together. I set out to fill those 365 pages with poetry. I had done this by the time I was eighteen, the summer after my junior year of college at Northwestern. I challenged my father then to say it was only a puberty urge. He laughed and said I would probably be writing poetry as long as I lived. Now in my seventh decade of life I am sad to think I do not write as much poetry as I wrote in my adolescence. Then I wrote almost every day—poetry, verse, or doggerel, I don't know which—but I wrote.

My father was also my first teacher of poetics. He said I must remember to include three elements in every poem: pictures or images; music or rhythm; and meaning. I think my parents were also my first sources of poetic inspiration. My mother's music, vocal and instrumental, gave me my only sense of rhythm. Whether the music was classical—Bach, Beethoven, and Brahms—church hymns or anthems, folk songs such as spirituals, work songs, blues, or ragtime and popular ballads and jazz, I heard music, my mother's music, as my earliest memory. My images have always come from the southern landscape of my childhood and adolescence. The meaning or philosophy came from my father, from his books and from his sermons. Most of all, it came from reading the Bible.

I attempted to write two long poems when I was in my teens. One I called "An Epic of the Dark Race" from Africa and slavery to segregation and the twentieth century. My mother, in her excitement, took that poem to Tuskegee to try to get it criticized and published. She gave me no time to copy it in my datebook, and I never saw or heard of it again. My mother also fell for a vanity publisher and paid to have four of my poems published. At Northwestern I was shamed into the knowledge that I should never do that again.

Eventually I came under the influence of sympathetic teachers other than my parents. My college freshman composition teacher, Miss Fluke, was a white woman teaching in a segregated black school in New Orleans. I was fifteen and I won the college freshman prize of five dollars. Miss Fluke told my father that I was head and shoulders above the rest of the class and that my parents should send me to a school where I would be more challenged. The next year, when I was sixteen, I met the famous young poet Langston Hughes. He read my poetry, said I had talent, and reiterated what Miss Fluke had said: "Get her out of the South so she can develop into a writer." Miss Fluke was a graduate of Northwestern and so was my father. That very summer after Mr. Hughes's visit in February, my parents took me, along with my sister Mercedes, a gifted musician and fifteen-year-old high school graduate, to Northwestern.

At Northwestern I met two men, one black and one white, who greatly influenced my life. Dr. W. E. B. Du Bois published my poetry for the first time in a national magazine, *Crisis,* when I was eighteen. Professor Edward Buell Hungerford, my favorite teacher at Northwestern, taught me in my senior year when I was nineteen (he also taught Saul Bellow and John Gardner). Professor Hungerford drilled me in types and forms of English prosody and made me seek to master versification and scansion. For his class in creative writing I wrote sixty-two typewritten pages of Keatsian run-on couplets about Jean Lafitte, the Baratarian pirate. I also wrote a short story called "Witches Eyes" in which I was swimming to the moon, and I began the novel *Jubilee* with three hundred typewritten pages. When Professor Hungerford hesitated over my grade after complimenting my work I asked him, "What do I have to do to make an 'A'?" He said my grade was "A." Persuaded by my poetry, Professor Hungerford had me admitted to the Northwestern chapter of the Poetry Society of America. I did not know until after I graduated what a fight he waged against racism to break down racial barriers for me.

At Northwestern I first heard of *Poetry, A Magazine of Verse,* and the Yale University Younger Poets competition. I heard Harriet Monroe read her poetry at Northwestern, and I must have seen an ad in the *Poets of America* magazine announcing the Yale competition. I vowed then to publish in *Poetry* and to enter the competition at Yale.

I graduated from Northwestern during the Depression, and after seven months looking for a job I began work on the WPA Chicago Writers' Project. Here I worked with Richard Wright, who was writing his first professional prose at the time. I was profoundly impressed with his talent, his intense driving ambition, his discipline, and his strange social theories and perspectives. The critic Robert Bone says Richard

Wright led a new movement, the Chicago Renaissance, which grew out of the South Side Writers' Group organized at that time. I was a member of that group for three years.

Meanwhile, I discovered that the office of *Poetry* was on the same street, Erie, as the Project where I worked. I met Miss Geraldine Udell, who introduced me to George Dillon, the editor of *Poetry* at that time. He encouraged me to read the French Symbolist poets. I could read both French and German and had already translated poems by Goethe, Schiller, and Heine. Now I was reading Baudelaire's *Les Fleurs du mal*, Rimbaud's *Une Saison en enfer*, Mallarmé's *L'Après-midi d'un faune*, and a smattering of Verlaine and Valéry. All my life I had read English and American classics, and I especially liked the English Romantic poets and American women writers such as Edna St. Vincent Millay, Léonie Adams, Elinor Wylie, and Louise Bogan. I met Muriel Rukeyser at a cocktail party at the office of *Poetry* just after she won the Yale award for *Theory of Flight*. It goes without saying that I had also read poetry by black people all my life: Langston Hughes, Countee Cullen, Claude McKay, Sterling Brown, and James Weldon Johnson. I was privileged to meet all of them.

Shortly after my twenty-second birthday I sat down at my typewriter and in fifteen minutes wrote all but the last stanza of the poem "For My People." Nelson Algren read it on the Project and told me how to write the resolution and conclusion. George Dillon published it that November in *Poetry.* The next year he published "We Have Been Believers" and the following year in a special WPA issue celebrating twenty-five years of *Poetry* he published my sonnet "The Struggle Staggers Us." In connection with the celebration there was a radio program and I was on that, too, reading my sonnet.

I had been trying to write sonnets since I was sixteen and seventeen. Professor Hungerford said poets have to write sonnets because sonnets furnish the same discipline for the poet as five-finger exercises for the musician. When I was in school in Iowa in the sixties I took my qualifying oral exam on sonnets, the history of that form, and sonnet sequences.

In Iowa in the late thirties, Paul Engle, my teacher in the poetry workshop and my thesis advisor, reawakened my interest in folk ballads and I began to experiment with that form. Also at Iowa I began to correspond with one of America's greatest balladeers, Stephen Vincent Benét. In 1942, five years after "For My People" was published and two years after the twenty-six poems in the *For My People* collection served as my master's thesis, I won the Yale award. *For My People* was published with a foreword by Mr. Benét.

I wrote "October Journey," a poem that has multiple meanings in my life, in 1943 after a few weeks at Yaddo, where I wrote the ballad "Harriet Tubman." I was actually making the journey South in October, and "October Journey" expresses my emotions at that time. I met my husband in October, and after thirty-seven years of our marriage he died in October. This poem was one of Arna Bontemps's favorites.

The decade of the sixties was a turbulent one in American society, and the civil rights confrontations made it a violent decade. The most violent year was 1963. By the time President Kennedy was assassinated in November, there had been many brutal killings in the South. Our neighbor Medgar Evers was assassinated on the street where I live. Four little girls were killed when Sixteenth Street Baptist Church in Birmingham was bombed. One of those children was the granddaughter of a neighbor from my childhood days in Birmingham. My cousins were members of Sixteenth Street Baptist Church, and they took me as a child to worship in that church. I gradually came to know many of the civil rights leaders, women and men, and so I was emotionally moved to write my civil rights poems in 1963. They are the poems in *Prophets for a New Day*.

One Sunday afternoon in 1963, ten years after my father died, I wrote ten typewritten pages of a poem called "Epitaph for My Father." That poem appeared in the *October Journey* collection. *Prophets for a New Day,* consisting of twenty-two poems in thirty-five pages, was published in 1970. Three years later in November 1973 the ten poems of the *October Journey* volume were published.

In 1979 I took early retirement from teaching at Jackson State University, where I had been since 1949. I immediately sat down and wrote the poems which constitute the section of this book called *This Is My Century.* Although twelve of the thirty poems in that section have seen previous publication, this is the first publication of the complete collection. In 1985 I was asked to write about Farish Street. The poems in *Farish Street,* the latest of the five sections, were printed in 1986.

All these poems have come out of my living. They express my ideas and emotions about being a woman and a black person in these United States—Land of the *Free* and Home of the Brave?

I seem to write in only three distinct forms: narratives or stories as ballads, lyrical songs as sonnets, and the long line of free verse punctuated with a short line. The characteristics of my poetry that may superficially be considered reflective of Sandburg, Masters, Jeffers, and Whitman are not derived from these poets but rather from a lifetime of reading the Bible and wisdom literature of the East—*Mahābhārata, Bhagavad-Gītā, Gilgamesh, Sundiata*—that they too had read. I have worn out four Bibles and am beginning to wear out the fifth. For twenty years I taught the Bible as literature at Jackson State University and for twenty-five years I taught the annual Bible study classes to the women in my local church. In my humanities classes I taught the wisdom literature of the East beginning with the *Book of the Dead* from Egypt; the *Mahābhārata* and *Bhagavad-Gītā* from India; *Gilgamesh* from

Babylonia; and the African epic *Sundiata*. All of these are pre-Homeric epics which my white professors denied existed.

Stephen Benét says I write my own kind of sonnet. My friends, the black male scholars and critics, speak disparagingly of my sonnets, but the editors of *The Sonnet: An Anthology,* Robert Bender and Charles Squier, say my sonnet on Malcolm X is one of the major sonnets of this century. Louis Untermeyer said my ballads were either Paul Laurence Dunbar gone modern or Langston Hughes gone sour. If I worried about what critics say I would stop trying to write, to practice the craft and the art of writing. As long as I live I shall keep trying. Why? Because I must.

I have lived most of my life in the segregated South. With the exception of one year in Meridian, Mississippi, when I was five, I lived in Birmingham, Alabama, my birthplace, until I was ten. I began writing in New Orleans, where I lived from age ten to seventeen. At seventeen I went out of the South for the first time to attend Northwestern University and, after graduation, lived and worked in Chicago for four years. I spent one year in the late thirties and three years in the sixties in Iowa, earning a master's degree in 1940 and a doctoral degree in 1965 from the University of Iowa. I began teaching at Livingstone College in North Carolina in 1941. After a year of teaching in West Virginia in 1942–43 I returned to North Carolina, where I married and resumed teaching. Since 1949 I have lived and worked in Jackson, Mississippi, going out of the South only to study, teach, or lecture. The South is my home, and my adjustment or accommodation to this South—whether real or imagined (mythic and legendary), violent or nonviolent—is the subject and source of all my poetry. It is also my life.

# ACKNOWLEDGMENTS

The author and publisher gratefully acknowledge the follow-ing publications in which many of these poems previously appeared:

*For My People*. New Haven: Yale University Press, 1942.
*Prophets for a New Day*. Detroit: Broadside Press, 1970.
*October Journey*. Detroit: Broadside Press, 1973.

"The Spirituals" and "Ex-Slave" were published in *Opportunity, A Journal of Negro Life* in 1938.

The poems in the "Farish Street" section were published in 1986 in the *Iowa Review* and the Jackson *Advocate*.

"This Is My Century," "Five Black Men," "My Truth and My Flame," "I Hear a Rumbling," and "Fanfare, Coda, and Fi-nale" appeared in Amiri Baraka (LeRoi Jones) and Amina Bar-aka, eds., *Confirmation: An Anthology of African American Women* (New York: William Morrow and Co., Inc., 1983).

"Birmingham 1963," "My Mississippi Spring," and "Black Paramour" were first published in *Southern Review*'s Afro-American special edition, 1986.

The following poems first appeared in *Black Scholar*: "Tribute to Robert Hayden" (1980), "Inflation Blues" (1980), "They Have Put Us on Hold" (1984), and "The Telly Boob-Tube on the Idiot Box" (1988–89).

# FOR MY PEOPLE

# FOREWORD TO *FOR MY PEOPLE*

For my playmates in the clay and dust and sand of Alabama
  backyards playing baptizing and preaching and doctor and jail
  and soldier and school and mama and cooking and playhouse
  and concert and store and hair and Miss Choomby and
  company;

For the cramped bewildered years we went to school to learn to
  know the reasons why and the answers to and the people who
  and the places where and the days when, in memory of the
  bitter hours when we discovered we were black and poor and
  small and different and nobody cared and nobody wondered
  and nobody understood;

. . . . . . . . . . . . . . . . . . . . . . . . . .

For my people thronging 47th Street in Chicago and Lenox
  Avenue in New York and Rampart Street in New Orleans,
  lost disinherited dispossessed and happy people filling the
  cabarets and taverns and other people's pockets needing bread
  and shoes and milk and land and money and something—
  something all our own.

It is unfair to pick three verses out of a connected and power-
ful poem—the title poem of this book. Yet they do give the
reader a taste of Miss Walker's quality. You will have to read
the whole poem to know its whole impact—and you should do
that. Straightforwardness, directness, reality are good things
to find in a young poet. It is rarer to find them combined with
a controlled intensity of emotion and a language that, at times,
even when it is most modern, has something of the surge of
biblical poetry. And it is obvious that Miss Walker uses that
language because it comes naturally to her and is part of
her inheritance. A contemporary writer, living in a contem-

porary world, when she speaks of and for her people older voices are mixed with hers—the voices of Methodist forebears and preachers who preached the Word, the anonymous voices of many who lived and were forgotten and yet out of bondage and hope made a lasting music. Miss Walker is not merely a sounding-board for these voices—I do not mean that. Nor do I mean that this is interesting and moving poetry because it was written by a Negro. It is too late in the day for that sort of meaningless patronage—and poetry must exist in its own right. These poems keep on talking to you after the book is shut because, out of deep feeling, Miss Walker has made living and passionate speech.

"We Have Been Believers," "Delta," "Southern Song," "For My People"—they are full of the rain and the sun that fall upon the faces and shoulders of her people, full of the bitter questioning and the answers not yet found, the pride and the disillusion and the reality. It is difficult for me to read these poems unmoved—I think it will be difficult for others. Yet it is not only the larger problems of her "playmates in the clay and dust" that interest Margaret Walker—she is interested in people wherever they are. In the second section of her book you will find ballads and portraits—figures of legend, like John Henry and Stagolee and the uncanny Molly Means—figures of realism like Poppa Chicken and Teacher and Gus, the Lineman, who couldn't die—figures "of Old Man River, round New Orleans, with her gumbo, rice, and good red beans." They are set for voice and the blues, they could be sung as easily as spoken. And, first and last, they are a part of our earth.

Miss Walker can write formal verse as well; she can write her own kind of sonnet. But, in whatever medium she is working, the note is true and unforced. There is a deep sincerity in all these poems—a sincerity at times disquieting. For this is what one American has found and seen—this is the song of her people, of her part of America. You cannot deny its honesty, you cannot deny its candor. And this is not far away or long ago—this is part of our nation, speaking.

I do not know what work Miss Walker will do in the future, though I should be very much surprised if this book were all she had to give. But I do know that, in this book, she has spoken of her people so that all may listen. I think that is something for any poet to have done.

Margaret Walker was born in Birmingham, Alabama, July 7, 1915. Her father is a Methodist minister, her mother a teacher of music. Both are university graduates. She has two sisters and a brother. Her early education took place in various church schools in Meridian, Mississippi; Birmingham, Alabama; and New Orleans, Louisiana. In 1935 she graduated from Northwestern University. For the next four years she worked in Chicago at various jobs—as typist, newspaper reporter, editor of a short-lived magazine, and on the Federal Writers Project. In 1939 she entered the School of Letters of the University of Iowa and received the degree of Master of Arts in 1940. She is now Professor of English at Livingstone College, Salisbury, North Carolina. She has written since she was thirteen, but *For My People* is her first published book.

Stephen Vincent Benét
1942

# FOR MY PEOPLE

For my people everywhere singing their slave songs
    repeatedly: their dirges and their ditties and their blues
    and jubilees, praying their prayers nightly to an
    unknown god, bending their knees humbly to an
    unseen power;

For my people lending their strength to the years, to the
    gone years and the now years and the maybe years,
    washing ironing cooking scrubbing sewing mending
    hoeing plowing digging planting pruning patching
    dragging along never gaining never reaping never
    knowing and never understanding;

For my playmates in the clay and dust and sand of Alabama
    backyards playing baptizing and preaching and doctor
    and jail and soldier and school and mama and cooking
    and playhouse and concert and store and hair and Miss
    Choomby and company;

For the cramped bewildered years we went to school to learn
    to know the reasons why and the answers to and the
    people who and the places where and the days when, in
    memory of the bitter hours when we discovered we
    were black and poor and small and different and nobody
    cared and nobody wondered and nobody understood;

For the boys and girls who grew in spite of these things to
    be man and woman, to laugh and dance and sing and
    play and drink their wine and religion and success, to
    marry their playmates and bear children and then die
    of consumption and anemia and lynching;

For my people thronging 47th Street in Chicago and Lenox
   Avenue in New York and Rampart Street in New
   Orleans, lost disinherited dispossessed and happy
   people filling the cabarets and taverns and other
   people's pockets needing bread and shoes and milk and
   land and money and something—something all our own;

For my people walking blindly spreading joy, losing time
   being lazy, sleeping when hungry, shouting when
   burdened, drinking when hopeless, tied, and shackled
   and tangled among ourselves by the unseen creatures
   who tower over us omnisciently and laugh;

For my people blundering and groping and floundering in
   the dark of churches and schools and clubs and
   societies, associations and councils and committees and
   conventions, distressed and disturbed and deceived and
   devoured by money-hungry glory-craving leeches,
   preyed on by facile force of state and fad and novelty, by
   false prophet and holy believer;

For my people standing staring trying to fashion a better way
   from confusion, from hypocrisy and misunderstanding,
   trying to fashion a world that will hold all the people,
   all the faces, all the adams and eves and their countless
   generations;

Let a new earth rise. Let another world be born. Let a
   bloody peace be written in the sky. Let a second
   generation full of courage issue forth; let a people
   loving freedom come to growth. Let a beauty full of
   healing and a strength of final clenching be the pulsing
   in our spirits and our blood. Let the martial songs be
   written, let the dirges disappear. Let a race of men now
   rise and take control.

# DARK BLOOD

There were bizarre beginnings in old lands for the making
    of me. There were sugar sands and islands of fern and
    pearl, palm jungles and stretches of a never-ending sea.

There were the wooing nights of tropical lands and the cool
    discretion of flowering plains between two stalwart
    hills. They nurtured my coming with wanderlust. I
    sucked fevers of adventure through my veins with my
    mother's milk.

Someday I shall go to the tropical lands of my birth, to the
    coasts of continents and the tiny wharves of island
    shores. I shall roam the Balkans and the hot lanes of
    Africa and Asia. I shall stand on mountain tops and
    gaze on fertile homes below.

And when I return to Mobile I shall go by the way of
    Panama and Bocas del Toro to the littered streets and
    the one-room shacks of my old poverty, and blazing suns
    of other lands may struggle then to reconcile the pride
    and pain in me.

# WE HAVE BEEN BELIEVERS

We have been believers believing in the black gods of an old
land, believing in the secrets of the seeress and the
magic of the charmers and the power of the devil's evil
ones.

And in the white gods of a new land we have been believers
believing in the mercy of our masters and the beauty of
our brothers, believing in the conjure of the humble
and the faithful and the pure.

Neither the slaves' whip nor the lynchers' rope nor the
bayonet could kill our black belief. In our hunger we
beheld the welcome table and in our nakedness the
glory of a long white robe. We have been believers in
the new Jerusalem.

We have been believers feeding greedy grinning gods, like a
Moloch demanding our sons and our daughters, our
strength and our wills and our spirits of pain. We have
been believers, silent and stolid and stubborn and
strong.

We have been believers yielding substance for the world.
With our hands have we fed a people and out of our
strength have they wrung the necessities of a nation.
Our song has filled the twilight and our hope has
heralded the dawn.

Now we stand ready for the touch of one fiery iron, for the
cleansing breath of many molten truths, that the eyes

of the blind may see and the ears of the deaf may hear
and the tongues of the people be filled with living fire.

Where are our gods that they leave us asleep? Surely the
priests and the preachers and the powers will hear.
Surely now that our hands are empty and our hearts too
full to pray they will understand. Surely the sires of
the people will send us a sign.

We have been believers believing in our burdens and our
demigods too long. Now the needy no longer weep and
pray; the long-suffering arise, and our fists bleed
against the bars with a strange insistency.

# SOUTHERN SONG

I want my body bathed again by southern suns, my soul
    reclaimed again from southern land. I want to rest
    again in southern fields, in grass and hay and clover
    bloom; to lay my hand again upon the clay baked by a
    southern sun, to touch the rain-soaked earth and smell
    the smell of soil.

I want my rest unbroken in the fields of southern earth;
    freedom to watch the corn wave silver in the sun and
    mark the splashing of a brook, a pond with ducks and
    frogs and count the clouds.

I want no mobs to wrench me from my southern rest; no
    forms to take me in the night and burn my shack and
    make for me a nightmare full of oil and flame.

I want my careless song to strike no minor key; no fiend to
    stand between my body's southern song—the fusion of
    the South, my body's song and me.

# SORROW HOME

My roots are deep in southern life; deeper than John Brown
    or Nat Turner or Robert Lee. I was sired and weaned
    in a tropic world. The palm tree and banana leaf,
    mango and coconut, breadfruit and rubber trees know
    me.

Warm skies and gulf blue streams are in my blood. I belong
    with the smell of fresh pine, with the trail of coon, and
    the spring growth of wild onion.

I am no hothouse bulb to be reared in steam-heated flats
    with the music of El and subway in my ears, walled in
    by steel and wood and brick far from the sky.

I want the cotton fields, tobacco and the cane. I want to
    walk along with sacks of seed to drop in fallow ground.
    Restless music is in my heart and I am eager to be
    gone.

O Southland, sorrow home, melody beating in my bone and
    blood! How long will the Klan of hate, the hounds and
    the chain gangs keep me from my own?

# THE SPIRITUALS

Yes these are ours . . . the spirituals
dark sons of moonless nights, bruised blood of
crushed and weak. Dig no grave to bury them—
these our children chained in grief.

Cotton pickers sing your song. Grumblers weed and
hoe the corn. Let the dirge of miners and
rebellious stirring road songs keep on ringing.

Mills of oppression grind songs of the poor.
Heels of the Moguls on necks of the humble
still click like castanets. And our sorrow
songs now rise to bolder measures, crashing
through crescendo into everlasting cadence. . . .

## EX-SLAVE

When I see you bending over something rare
    Like music, or a painting, or a book,
    And see within your eyes that vacant stare
    And halfway understand that pleading look;
    I cannot help but bitterly detest
    The age and men who made you what you are,
    Who robbed you of your all—your ample best—
    And left you seeking life across a hateful bar,
    And left you vainly searching for a star
    Your soul appreciates but cannot understand.

# DELTA

## I

I am a child of the valley.
Mud and muck and misery of lowlands
are on thin tracks of my feet.
Damp draughts of mist and fog hovering over valleys
are on my feverish breath.
Red clay from feet of beasts colors my mouth
and there is blood on my tongue.

I go up and down and through this valley
and my heart bleeds for our fate.
I turn to each stick and stone, marking them for
     my own;
here where muddy water flows at our shanty door
and levees stand like a swollen bump on our
     backyard.

I watch rivulets flow
trickling into one great river
running through little towns
through swampy thickets and smoky cities
through fields of rice and marshes
where the marsh hen comes to stand
and buzzards draw thin blue streaks against evening
     sky.
I listen to crooning of familiar lullabies;
the honky-tonks are open and the blues are ringing
     far.
In cities a thousand red lamps glow,

but the lights fail to stir me
and the music cannot lift me
and my despair only deepens with the wailing of a million
    voices strong.


O valley of my moaning brothers!
Valley of my sorrowing sisters!
Valley of lost forgotten men.
O hunted desperate people
stricken and silently submissive
seeking yet sullen ones!
If only from this valley we might rise with song!
With singing that is ours.


## II


Here in this valley of cotton and cane and banana
    wharves
we labor.
Our mothers and fathers labored before us
here in this low valley.


High above us and round about us stand high
    mountains
rise the towering snow-capped mountains
while we are beaten and broken and bowed
here in this dark valley.


The river passes us by.
Boats slip by on the edge of horizons.

Daily we fill boats with cargoes of our need
and send them out to sea.

Orange and plantain and cotton grow
here in this wide valley.
Wood fern and sour grass and wild onion grow
here in this sweet valley.

We tend the crop and gather the harvest
but not for ourselves do we labor,
not for ourselves do we sweat and starve and spend
under these mountains we dare not claim,
here on this earth we dare not claim,
here by the river we dare not claim.
Yet we are an age of years in this valley;
yet we are bound till death to this valley.

Nights in the valley are full of haunting murmurings
of our musical prayers
of our rhythmical loving
of our fumbling thinking aloud.
Nights in the houses of our miserable poor
are wakeful and tormenting,
for out of a deep slumber we are 'roused
to our brother who is ill
and our sister who is ravished
and our mother who is starving.
Out of a deep slumber truth rides upon us
and we wonder why we are helpless
and we wonder why we are dumb.
Out of a deep slumber truth rides upon us
and makes us restless and wakeful
and full of a hundred unfulfilled dreams of today;
our blood eats through our veins with the terrible destruction

of radium in our bones and rebellion in our brains
and we wish no longer to rest.


## III


Now burst the dams of years
and winter snows melt with an onrush of a turbulent
      spring.
Now rises sap in slumbering elms
and floods overwhelm us
here in this low valley.
Here there is a thundering sound in our ears.
All the day we are disturbed;
nothing ever moved our valley more.
The cannons boom in our brains
and there is a dawning understanding
in the valleys of our spirits;
there is a crystalline hope
there is a new way to be worn and a path to be broken
from the past


Into our troubled living flows the valley
flooding our lives with a passion for freedom.
Our silence is broken in twain
even as brush is broken before terrible rain
even as pines rush in paths of hurricanes.
Our blood rises and bursts in great heart spasms
hungering down through valleys in pain
and the storm begins.
We are dazed in wonder and caught in the downpour.
Danger and death stalk the valley.

Robbers and murderers rape the valley
taking cabins and children from us
seeking to threaten us out of this valley.

Then with a longing dearer than breathing
love for the valley arises within us
love to possess and thrive in this valley
love to possess our vineyards and pastures
our orchards and cattle
our harvest of cotton, tobacco, and cane.
Love overwhelms our living with longing
strengthening flesh and blood within us
banding the iron of our muscles with anger
making us men in the fields we have tended
standing defending the land we have rendered
rich and abiding and heavy with plenty.

We with our blood have watered these fields
and they belong to us.
Valleys and dust of our bodies are blood brothers
and they belong to us:
the long golden grain for bread
and the ripe purple fruit for wine
the hills beyond for peace
and the grass beneath for rest
the music in the wind for us
the nights for loving
the days for living
and the circling lines in the sky
for dreams.

We are like the sensitive Spring
walking valleys like a slim young girl
full breasted and precious limbed

and carrying on our lips the kiss of the world.
Only the naked arm of Time
can measure the ground we know
and thresh the air we breathe.
Neither earth nor star nor water's host
can sever us from our life to be
for we are beyond your reach O mighty winnowing flail!
infinite and free!

# LINEAGE

My grandmothers were strong.
They followed plows and bent to toil.
They moved through fields sowing seed.
They touched earth and grain grew.
They were full of sturdiness and singing.
My grandmothers were strong.

My grandmothers are full of memories
Smelling of soap and onions and wet clay
With veins rolling roughly over quick hands
They have many clean words to say.
My grandmothers were strong.
Why am I not as they?

# SINCE 1619

How many years since 1619 have I been singing Spirituals?
How long have I been praising God and shouting hallelujahs?
How long have I been hated and hating?
How long have I been living in hell for heaven?

When will I see my brother's face wearing another color?
When will I be ready to die in a honest fight?
When will I be conscious of the struggle—now to do or die?
When will these scales fall away from my eyes?

What will I say when days of wrath descend:
When the money-gods take all my life away;
When the death knell sounds
And peace is a flag of far-flung blood and filth?

When will I understand the cheated and the cheaters;
Their paltry pittances and cold concessions to my pride?
When will I burst from my kennel an angry mongrel,
Lean and hungry and tired of my dry bones and years?

# PEOPLE OF UNREST

Stare from your pillow into the sun.
See the disk of light in shadows.
Watch day grow tall.
Cry with a loud voice after the sun.
Take his yellow arms and wrap them round your life.
Be glad to be washed in the sun.
Be glad to see.
People of unrest and sorrow
Stare from your pillow into the sun.

# TODAY

## I

I sing of slum scabs on city faces, scrawny children scarred by bombs and dying of hunger, wretched human scarecrows strung against lynching stakes, those dying of pellagra and silicosis, rotten houses falling on slowly decaying humanity.

I sing of Man's struggle to be clean, to be useful, to be free; of need arising from our lives, of bitter living flowing in our laughter, of cankerous mutiny eating through the nipples of our breasts.

I sing of our soon-to-be-dead, of last escape: drunkard raising flasks to his lips never tasting the solace, gambler casting his last die never knowing the win, lover seeking lips of the beloved never tasting fruit of his kiss, never knowing the languorous sleep.

I sing these fragments of living that you may know by these presents that which we feared most has come upon us.

## II

You walking these common neighboring streets with no disturbing drone of bombing planes, no Sunday air-raiding, and no shells caving in roofs of your houses; fearing no severed baby arms nor naked

eyeballs hurtled in your hands; riding trolley and jitney
daily, buying gas and light hourly, viewing weekly "Wild
West Indian and Shooting Sam," "Mama Loves Papa," and
"Gone by the Breeze," complacently smug in a snug
somnolescence;

                        You in Middle America
distantly removed from Middle Europe, no closer than
morning headlines and evening news flashes, bothered by
petty personals—your calories and eyemaline, your henna
rinse and dental cream, washing your lives with pity,
smoothing your ways with vague apologies;

                        Pray the Men of Mars to
descend upon you. Pray Jehovah to send his prophets before
the avenging fire. Pray for second sight and inner ear. Pray
for bulwark against poaching patterns of dislocated days;
pray for buttressing iron against insidious termite and beetle
and locust and flies and lice and moth and rust and mold.

# MOLLY MEANS

Old Molly Means was a hag and a witch;
Chile of the devil, the dark, and sitch.
Her heavy hair hung thick in ropes
And her blazing eyes was black as picch.
Imp at three and wench at 'leben
She counted her husbands to the number seben.
   O Molly, Molly, Molly Means
   There goes the ghost of Molly Means.

Some say she was born with a veil on her face
So she could look through unnatural space
Through the future and through the past
And charm a body or an evil place
And every man could well despise
The evil look in her coal black eyes.
   Old Molly, Molly, Molly Means
   Dark is the ghost of Molly Means.

And when the tale begun to spread
Of evil and of holy dread:
Her black-hand arts and her evil powers
How she could cast her spells and called the dead,
The younguns was afraid at night
And the farmers feared their crops would blight.
   Old Molly, Molly, Molly Means
   Cold is the ghost of Molly Means.

Then one dark day she put a spell
On a young gal-bride just come to dwell
In the lane just down from Molly's shack

And when her husband come riding back
His wife was barking like a dog
And on all fours like a common hog.
   O Molly, Molly, Molly Means
   Where is the ghost of Molly Means?


The neighbors come and they went away
And said she'd die before break of day
But her husband held her in his arms
And swore he'd break the wicked charms;
He'd search all up and down the land
And turn the spell on Molly's hand.
   O Molly, Molly, Molly Means
   Sharp is the ghost of Molly Means.


So he rode all day and he rode all night
And at the dawn he come in sight
Of a man who said he could move the spell
And cause the awful thing to dwell
On Molly Means, to bark and bleed
Till she died at the hands of her evil deed.
   Old Molly, Molly, Molly Means
   This is the ghost of Molly Means.


Sometimes at night through the shadowy trees
She rides along on a winter breeze.
You can hear her holler and whine and cry.
Her voice is thin and her moan is high,
And her cackling laugh or her barking cold
Bring terror to the young and old.
   O Molly, Molly, Molly Means
   Lean is the ghost of Molly Means.

# BAD-MAN STAGOLEE*

That Stagolee was an all-right lad
Till he killed a cop and turned out bad,
Though some do say to this very day
He killed more'n one 'fore he killed that 'fay.
But anyhow the tale ain't new
How Stagolee just up and slew
A big policeman on 'leventh street
And all he knowed was tweet-tweet-tweet
Oh I 'speck he'd done some too-bad dirt
Wid dat blade he wore unnerneaf his shirt
And it ain't been said, but he coulda had
A dirk in his pocket 'cause he sho was bad
But one thing's certain and two things's sho
His bullets made holes no doc could cyo.
And that there cop was good and done
When he met Stagolee and that blue boy's gun.
But the funniest thing about that job
Was he never got caught by no mob
And he missed the lynching meant for his hide
'Cause nobody knows how Stagolee died.
Bad-Man Stagolee ain't no more
But his ghost still walks up and down the shore
Of Old Man River round New Orleans
With her gumbo, rice, and good red beans!

*Pronounced Stack'-a-lee.

# POPPA CHICKEN

Poppa was a sugah daddy
Pimping in his prime;
All the gals for miles around
Walked to Poppa's time.

Poppa Chicken owned the town,
Give his women hell;
All the gals on Poppa's time
Said that he was swell.

Poppa's face was long and black;
Poppa's grin was broad.
When Poppa Chicken walked the streets
The gals cried Lawdy! Lawd!

Poppa Chicken made his gals
Toe his special line:
"Treat 'em rough and make 'em say
Poppa Chicken's fine!"

Poppa Chicken toted guns;
Poppa wore a knife.
One night Poppa shot a guy
Threat'ning Poppa's life.

Poppa done his time in jail
Though he got off light;

Bought his pardon in a year;
Come back out in might.

Poppa walked the streets this time,
Gals around his neck.
And everybody said the jail
Hurt him nary speck.

Poppa smoked his long cigars—
Special Poppa brands—
Rocks all glist'ning in his tie;
On his long black hands.

Poppa lived without a fear;
Walked without a rod.
Poppa cussed the coppers out;
Talked like he was God.

Poppa met a pretty gal;
Heard her name was Rose;
Took one look at her and soon
Bought her pretty clothes.

One night she was in his arms,
In walked her man Joe.
All he done was look and say,
"Poppa's got to go."

Poppa Chicken still is hot
Though he's old and gray,
Walking round here with his gals
Pimping every day.

# KISSIE LEE

Toughest gal I ever did see
Was a gal by the name of Kissie Lee;
The toughest gal God ever made
And she drew a dirty, wicked blade.

Now this here gal warn't always tough
Nobody dreamed she'd turn out rough
But her Grammaw Mamie had the name
Of being the town's sin and shame.

When Kissie Lee was young and good
Didn't nobody treat her like they should
Allus gettin' beat by a no-good shine
An' allus quick to cry and whine.

Till her Grammaw said, "Now listen to me,
I'm tiahed of yoah whinin', Kissie Lee.
People don't ever treat you right,
An' you allus scrappin' or in a fight."

"Whin I was a gal wasn't no soul
Could do me wrong an' still stay whole.
Ah got me a razor to talk for me
An' aftah that they let me be."

Well Kissie Lee took her advice
And after that she didn't speak twice

'Cause when she learned to stab and run
She got herself a little gun.

And from that time that gal was mean,
Meanest mama you ever seen.
She could hold her likker and hold her man
And she went thoo life jus' raisin' san'.

One night she walked in Jim's saloon
And seen a guy what spoke too soon;
He done her dirt long time ago
When she was good and feeling low.

Kissie bought her drink and she paid her dime
Watchin' this guy what beat her time
And he was making for the outside door
When Kissie shot him to the floor.

Not a word she spoke but she switched her blade
And flashing that lil ole baby paid:
Evvy livin' guy got out of her way
Because Kissie Lee was drawin' her pay.

She could shoot glass offa the hinges,
She could take herself on the wildest binges.
And she died with her boots on switching blades
On Talladega Mountain in the likker raids.

# YALLUH HAMMUH

Old Yalluh Hammuh were a guy
I knowed long time ago.
I seen him pile the san'bags high
An' holler back fuh moah.


I seen him come on inta town
Many a Saddy night
Ridin' high with his jive
An' clownin' leff an' right.


They wasn't no sheriffs near or far
Would dare to 'rest dat man;
An' las' I heerd they wanted him
For two-t'ree county cans.


Old Yalluh Hammuh lay his jive
On mens on every side
And when it come to women folks
His fame was far and wide.


Now Yalluh Hammuh was so bad
He killed his Maw of fright
He swaggered through the county seat
All full of lip and might.


But Yalluh Hammuh met his match
One Saddy night, they say,

He come in town an' run into
Pick-Ankle's gal named May.

Pick-Ankle now was long and lean
An' some say he was mean,
An' if you touched his brown gal, May,
His eyes turned fairly green.

Well this time Yalluh Hammuh's jive
Went to town wid his pay;
He went on in a lil shindig
An' spied Pick-Ankle's May.

He ax huh to dance; she excep;
And then he went to town.
The crowd went wild till here come Pick
And then they quieted down.

But Yalluh Hammuh don't ketch on
Ole May was having fun
Till Pick comes up and calls huh names
Then Yalluh drawed his gun.

The lights went out and womens screamed
And then they fit away.
When Yalluh Hammuh come to hisself
May was gone with his pay.

# TWO-GUN BUSTER
# AND TRIGGER SLIM

Two-Gun Buster was a railroad han'
Splittin' ties in the backwoods lan'
Cuttin' logs and layin' down rails,
Blazin' out the iron horse trails.

Biggest bluff an' cockiest cuss
Two-Gun never had no fuss
'Cause all the hands was frightened dead
At Two-Gun's handy way with lead.

Two-Gun Buster got his fame
Same sorter way he got his name
Carryin' them two guns in his ves'
An' scarin' all the mens at mess.

He had a belly he couldn't fill
With what the cook had on the bill
An' wasn't no second plates allowed
So Two-Gun had the mens all cowed.

An' when he finished with his grub
He made the rest fill up his tub
He riz and opened up his ves'
An' walked the tables in the mess.

The mens drawed back an' give in to him
Until the Lil Lad cured his whim

'Cause then when Two-Gun started his stuff
That Lil Lad just called his bluff.

Lil Lad looked as green as grass
But he had nerve like brazen brass;
He split them ties like kin'lin' wood.
He sho did earn his plate of food.

At supper time he looked around
When suddenly there warnt a sound
Two-Gun Buster was eatin' a bait
Comin' on down to Lil Lad's plate.

He stuck his fork in Lil Lad's meat
An' Lil Lad rose right to his feet
He grabbed old Two-Gun in a vise
An' axed his meanin' in that wise.

Two-Gun went to draw his steel
But Lil Lad shot him in a reel
Sprawlin' on the mess hall floor
An' all the mens falls out the door.

Lil Lad finish his dinner plate
An' walks on through the camp's big gate;
Don't say no word, an' stayed away;
He didn't come back to draw his pay.

But from that time they made a claim
That they had heerd of him
So they give the Lil Lad a name
And they called him Trigger Slim.

# TEACHER

The Teacher was a bad man
    Not a milky-mild
Student with a book or rule
    Punishing a child.

Teacher was a pimp, a rake;
    Teacher was a card.
Teacher had a gambling den
    Down on St. Girod.

Teacher liked his liquor strong;
    Drank his dry gin straight.
Teacher hung around the Tracks
    Catching juicy bait.

Teacher was as black as Aces
    Of a brand new spade.
Teacher's lust included all
    Women ever made.

Teacher's women drove him nuts;
    Led him such a chase
He was stealing extra cash
    For each pretty face.

Women scarred his upper lip;
    Nearly tore his head

Off his shoulders with a gun
   Kept his eyes blood-red.

Women sent him to his doom.
   Women set the trap.
Teacher was a bad, bold man
   Lawd, but such a sap!

# GUS, THE LINEMAN

Gus, the lineman,
Route forty-nine;
Our smartest guy.
Had a smart line.

He had nine lives
And lived them all.
He climbed the trees
From Fall to Fall.

He handled juice
Whistling a tune;
Chewed tobacco
And drank bad moon.

Once on his job
Pains in his side
Said call the doc
Or take a ride.

And in the Ward
They said his side
Was so bad off
He should have died.

But Gus come through
Living the Life

Back on the job
'Spite of that knife.


The juice went wild
And great big chunks
Of flesh caught fire
And fell in hunks.


But Gus outlived
That little fire.
He soon was back
Handling live wire.


It got around
Gus could not die
He'd lived through death
And come through fire.


One Saddy night
Old Gus got high
Drinking moonshine
And good old Rye.


He staggered home
In pitch-black night
And swayed along
From left to right.


He fell into
A little crick

And went out dead
Just like a brick.

They found him drowned
Face in the stream
A cup of water
And his drunk dream.

And thus went down
A mighty guy—
Gus, the lineman,
Who could not die.

# LONG JOHN NELSON AND SWEETIE PIE

Long John Nelson and Sweetie Pie
Lived together on Center Street.
Long John was a mellow fellow
And Sweetie Pie was fat and sweet.

Long John Nelson had been her man
Long before this story began;
Sweetie cooked on the Avenue.
Long John's loving was all he'd do.

When Sweetie Pie came home at night
She brought his grub and fed him well
Then she would fuss and pick a fight
Till he beat her and gave her hell.

She would cuss and scream, call him black
Triflin' man git outa my sight;
Then she would love him half the night
And when he'd leave she'd beg him back.

Till a yellow gal came to town
With coal black hair and bright blue gown
And she took Long John clean away
From Sweetie Pie one awful day.

Sweetie begged him to please come back
But Long John said, "I'm gone to stay."

Then Sweetie Pie would moan and cry
And sing the blues both night and day:

"Long John, Baby, if you'll come back
I won't never call you black;
I'll love you long and love you true
And I don't care what else you do."

But Long John said, "I'm really through."
They're still apart this very day.
When Long John got a job to do
Sweetie got sick and wasted away.

Then after she had tried and tried
One day Sweetie just up and died.
Then Long John went and quit his job
And up and left his yellow bride.

# BIG JOHN HENRY

This here's a tale of a sho-nuff man
Whut lived one time in the delta lan'
His hand was big as a hog's fat ham
And he useta work for Uncle Sam.
His gums was blue, his voice was mellow
And he talked to mules, fellow to fellow.
The day he was born in the Mississippi
      bottom
He made a meal on buttermilk and sorghum
A mess o' peas and a bait o' tunnips
And when he finished he smacked his lips
And went outside to help pick cotton.
And he growed up taller than a six-foot
      shooter
Skinnin' mules and catchin' barracuda
And stronger than a team of oxen
And he even could beat the champion
      boxin'
An' ain't nary man in Dixie's forgotten
How he could raise two bales of cotton
While one hand anchored down the
      steamboat.
Oh, they ain't no tale was ever wrote
'Bout Big John Henry that could start to tell
All the things that Big Boy knowed so well:
How he learned to whistle from the
      whippoorwills,
And turned the wheels whut ran the mills;
How the witches taught him how to cunjer,
And cyo the colic and ride the thunder;

And how he made friends with a long lean
      houn'
Sayin', "It's jes' John Henry a-giftin' roun'."
But a ten-poun' hammer done ki-ilt John Henry
Yeah, a ten-poun' hammer ki-ilt John Henry,
Bust him open, wide Lawd!
Drapped him ovah, wide Lawd!
Po' John Henry, he cold and dead.

# CHILDHOOD

When I was a child I knew red miners
dressed raggedly and wearing carbide lamps.
I saw them come down red hills to their camps
dyed with red dust from old Ishkooda mines.
Night after night I met them on the roads,
or on the streets in town I caught their glance;
the swing of dinner buckets in their hands,
and grumbling undermining all their words.

I also lived in low cotton country
where moonlight hovered over ripe haystacks,
or stumps of trees, and croppers' rotting shacks
with famine, terror, flood, and plague near by;
where sentiment and hatred still held sway
and only bitter land was washed away.

# WHORES

When I grew up I went away to work
where painted whores were fascinating sights.
They came on like whole armies through the nights—
their sullen eyes on mine, their mouths a smirk,
and from their hands keys hung suggestively.
Old women working by an age-old plan
to make their bread in ways as best they can
would hobble past and beckon tirelessly.

Perhaps one day they'll all die in the streets
or be surprised by bombs in each wide bed;
learning too late in unaccustomed dread
that easy ways, like whores on special beats,
no longer have the gift to harbor pride
or bring men peace, or leave them satisfied.

# IOWA FARMER

I talked to a farmer one day in Iowa.
We looked out far over acres of wheat.
He spoke with pride and yet not boastfully;
he had no need to fumble for his words.
He knew his land and there was love for home
within the soft serene eyes of his son.
His ugly house was clean against the storm;
there was no hunger deep within the heart
nor burning riveted within the bone,
but there they ate a satisfying bread.
Yet in the Middle West where wheat was plentiful;
where grain grew golden under sunny skies
and cattle fattened through the summer heat
I could remember more familiar sights.

# MEMORY

I can remember wind-swept streets of cities
on cold and blustery nights, on rainy days;
heads under shabby felts and parasols
and shoulders hunched against a sharp concern;
seeing hurt bewilderment on poor faces,
smelling a deep and sinister unrest
these brooding people cautiously caress;
hearing ghostly marching on pavement stones
and closing fast around their squares of hate.
I can remember seeing them alone,
at work, and in their tenements at home.
I can remember hearing all they said:
their muttering protests, their whispered oaths,
and all that spells their living distress.

# OUR NEED

If dead men died abruptly by a blow—
startled and trapped in today's immediacy,
having neither moments to speak dazedly
nor whimper wistfully—how can they know
or tell us now the way which we should go?
What price upon their wisdom can we stake
if ultimately we would live, not break
beneath a swift and dangerous undertow?

We need a wholeness born of inner strength:
sharp thinking running through our stream of days,
having certain courage flame with honest rays
like slaps of life along the body's length.
We need the friendly feel of human forms
and earth beneath our feet against the storms.

# THE STRUGGLE STAGGERS US

Our birth and death are easy hours, like sleep
and food and drink. The struggle staggers us
for bread, for pride, for simple dignity.
And this is more than fighting to exist;
more than revolt and war and human odds.
There is a journey from the me to you.
There is a journey from the you to me.
A union of the two strange worlds must be.

Ours is a struggle from a too-warm bed;
too cluttered with a patience full of sleep.
Out of this blackness we must struggle forth;
from want of bread, of pride, of dignity.
Struggle between the morning and the night.
This marks our years; this settles, too, our plight.

# PROPHETS
# FOR A NEW DAY

# STREET DEMONSTRATION

*Hurry up Lucille or we won't get arrested with our group.*

An eight-year-old demonstrator, 1963

We're hoping to be arrested
And hoping to go to jail
We'll sing and shout and pray
For Freedom and for Justice
And for Human Dignity
The Fighting may be long
And some of us will die
But Liberty is costly
And ROME they say to me
Was not built in one day.

*Hurry up, Lucille, Hurry up*
*We're Going to Miss Our Chance to go to Jail.*

# GIRL HELD WITHOUT BAIL

*In an unjust state the only place*
*for a just man is in jail.*

I like it here just fine
And I don't want no bail
My sister's here
My mother's here
An all my girlfriends too.
I want my rights
I'm fighting for my rights
I want to be treated
Just like *anybody* else
I want to be treated
Just like *everybody* else

*I like it fine in Jail*
*And I don't want no Bail.*

# NOW

Time to wipe away the slime
from inner rooms of thinking,
and covert skin of suffering;
indignities and dirt
and helpless degradation;
from furtive relegation
to the back doors and dark alleys
and the balconies of waiting
in the cleaning rooms and closets
with the washrooms and the filthy
privies marked "For Colored Only"
and the drinking-soda-fountains
tasting dismal and disgusting
with a dry and dusty flavor
of the deep humiliation;
hearing vulgars shout to mothers
"Hey you, nigger girl, and girlie!
Auntie, Ant, and Granny;
My old mammy was a wonder
and I love those dear old darkies
who were good and servile nigras
with their kerchiefed heads and faces
in their sweet and menial places."
Feeling hate and blood comingled
in a savage supplication
full of rites and ceremonies
for the separate unequal—
re-enforced by mobs who mass
with a priest of cult and klan
robed and masked in purest White

marking Kleagle with a Klux
and a fiery burning cross.
Time to wipe away the slime.
Time to end this bloody crime.

# SIT-INS

*Greensboro, North Carolina, in the Spring of 1960*


You were our first brave ones to defy their dissonance of hate
With your silence
With your willingness to suffer
Without violence
Those first bright young to fling your names across pages
Of new southern history
With courage and faith, convictions, and intelligence
The first to blaze a flaming path for justice
And awaken consciences
Of these stony ones.

*Come, Lord Jesus, Bold Young Galilean*
*Sit Beside this Counter, Lord, with Me!*

# THE BALLAD OF THE FREE

Bold Nat Turner by the blood of God
Rose up Preaching on Virginia's sod;
Smote the land with his passionate plea
Time's done come to set my people free.

    The serpent is loosed and the hour is come
    The last shall be first and first shall be none
    The serpent is loosed and the hour is come

Gabriel Prosser looked at the sun,
Said, "Sun, stand still till the work is done.
The world is wide and the time is long
And man must meet the avenging wrong."

    The serpent is loosed and the hour is come
    The last shall be first and first shall be none
    The serpent is loosed and the hour is come

Denmark Vesey led his band
Across the hot Carolina land.
The plot was foiled, the brave men killed,
But Freedom's cry was never stilled.

    The serpent is loosed and the hour is come
    The last shall be first and first shall be none
    The serpent is loosed and the hour is come

Toussaint L'Ouverture won
All his battles in the tropic sun,

*Hero of the black man's pride*
*Among those hundred who fought and died.*

   The serpent is loosed and the hour is come
   The last shall be first and first shall be none
   The serpent is loosed and the hour is come

*Brave John Brown was killed but he*
*Became a martyr of the free,*
*For he declared that blood would run*
*Before the slaves their freedom won.*

   The serpent is loosed and the hour is come
   The last shall be first and first shall be none
   The serpent is loosed and the hour is come

*Wars and Rumors of Wars have gone,*
*But Freedom's army marches on.*
*The heroes' list of dead is long,*
*And Freedom still is for the strong.*

   The serpent is loosed and the hour is come
   The last shall be first and first shall be none
   The serpent is loosed and the hour is come

# JACKSON, MISSISSIPPI

City of tense and stricken faces
City of closed doors and ketchup-splattered floors,
City of barbed wire stockades,
And ranting voices of demagogues,
City of squealers and profane voices;
Hauling my people in garbage trucks,
Fenced in by new white police billies,
Fist cuffs and red-necked brothers of Hate Legions
Straining their leashed and fiercely hungry dogs;
City of tree-lined, wide, white avenues
And black alleys of filthy rendezvous;
City of flowers: of new red zinnias
And oriental poppies and double-ruffled petunias
Ranch styled houses encircled with rose geranium
And scarlet salvia
And trouble-ridden minds of the guilty and the
        conscienceless;
City of stooges and flunkeys, pimps and prostitutes,
Barflies and railroad-station freaks;
City with southern sun beating down raw fire
On heads of blaring jukes,
And light-drenched streets puddled with the promise
Of a brand-new tomorrow
I give you my heart, Southern City
For you are my blood and dust of my flesh,
You are the harbor of my ship of hope,
The dead-end street of my life,
And the long washed down drain of my youth's years of toil,
In the bosom of your families
I have planted my seeds of dreams and visions and prophecies

All my fantasies of freedom and of pride,
Here lie three centuries of my eyes and my brains and my
    hands,
Of my lips and strident demands,
The graves of my dead,
And the birthing stools of grannies long since fled.
Here are echoes of my laughing children
And hungry minds of pupils to be fed.
I give you my brimming heart, Southern City
For my eyes are full and no tears cry
And my throat is dusty and dry.

# OXFORD IS A LEGEND

OXFORD is a legend
Where battlements were placed
One flaming night
And they fought the civil war all over again
With a rebel yell, and rebel flag, and scholars yelling "nigger,"
A Confederate general,
And the Union army;
Where innocent bystanders
Were killed.

OXFORD is a legend
Only a state of mind
And a place in Yoknapatawpha
Too bad the old man from Jefferson County
Died before he saw the fighting in his streets
Before he had to bear arms for Mississippi
And shoot the Negroes in the streets.

OXFORD is a legend
Name of a town in England
University town in England and Ohio and Mississippi
Where all the bygone years of chivalry and poetry and
        crinoline
Are dead.

OXFORD is a legend
Out of time more than battle place, or a name
With the figure of one brave and smiling little man
Smiling that courageous, ironic, bright, grim smile
Smile of a black American.

# BIRMINGHAM

## I

With the last whippoorwill call of evening
Settling over mountains
Dusk dropping down shoulders of red hills
And red dust of mines
Sifting across somber sky
Setting the sun to rest in a blue blaze of coal fire
And shivering memories of Spring
With raw wind out of woods
And brown straw of last year's needle-shedding-pines
Cushions of quiet underfoot
Violets pushing through early new spring ground
And my winging heart flying across the world
With one bright bird—
Cardinal flashing through thickets—
Memories of my fancy-ridden life
Come home again.

## II

I died today.
In a new and cruel way.
I came to breakfast in my night-dying clothes
Ate and talked and nobody knew
They had buried me yesterday.
I slept outside city limits
Under a little hill of butterscotch brown
With a dusting of white sugar

Where a whistling ghost kept making a threnody
Out of a naked wind.

## III

Call me home again to my coffin bed of soft warm clay.
I cannot bear to rest in frozen wastes
Of a bitter cold and sleeting northern womb.
My life dies best on a southern cross
Carved out of rock with shooting stars to fire
The forge of bitter hate.

# HOW MANY SILENT CENTURIES
# SLEEP IN MY SULTRY VEINS?

How many silent centuries sleep in my sultry veins?
The cries of tribal dancers call from far-off buried plains;
The plaintive songs of India, the melodies of Spain;
The rhythms of their tom-tom drums;
Of Red men seeking southern lands,
Of Africans in chains.
They call me from their tombs and thrones;
From many distant climes;
They whisper old and sacred names:
Each intonation chimes
An ancient and familiar rite
For primitive and erudite.
I hear them wail loud echoings.
Locked deep inside of me they cry—
And wild their clamorings!
Blood rituals of men and gods
Speak pitiless, and shriek.
And crashing barriers of time
These dark imprisoned sons
Of all my wild ancestral hosts
Break from their time-locked sea
To make these modern, sensate sons
Immortal men, and free.

# AT THE
# LINCOLN MONUMENT
# IN WASHINGTON,
# AUGUST 28, 1963

There they stand together, like Moses standing with Aaron;
Whose rod is in his hand,
The old man Moses standing with his younger brother,
    Aaron,
Old man with a dream he has lived to see come true.
And that firebrand standing close at hand,
Stretching forth a rod across the land,
Leading his people forth with Aaron at his side
In their marching out of Egypt,
To—the Red Sea
With the East wind sweeping back a Tide
Of the hosts of Pharaoh.
We woke up one morning in Egypt
And the river ran red with blood;
We woke up one morning in Egypt
And the houses of death were afraid.
Now the leaders of the marchers
Stand and count the uncountable;
Jacob's house has grown into a Nation.
The slaves break forth from bondage,
And there are with them intermingled
All the wives and children of other nations,
All the heathen marriages with the peoples of the land;
They march out of Goshen
They overflow out of Egypt
The Red Sea cannot stop them

And here in the wilderness of a century of wandering
Where shall we lead them
If not to freedom?

So the leaders of the marchers
Stand and catechize the people
Write this word upon your hearts
And mark this message on the doors of your houses
See that you do not forget
How this day the Lord has set our faces toward Freedom
Teach these words to your children
And see that they do not forget them.
Recite them in your going out and your coming in
And speak them in the silence of the night.
Remember the covenant we have made together
Here in the eyes of our Liberator
Here in the witnessing presence of our God and fellowman.
Where shall we march
If not to Freedom
And to our Promised Land?

# FOR MALCOLM X

All you violated ones with gentle hearts;
You violent dreamers whose cries shout heartbreak;
Whose voices echo clamors of our cool capers,
And whose black faces have hollowed pits for eyes.
All you gambling sons and hooked children and bowery
        bums
Hating white devils and black bourgeoisie,
Thumbing your noses at your burning red suns,
Gather round this coffin and mourn your dying swan.

Snow-white moslem head-dress around a dead black face!
Beautiful were your sand-papering words against our skins!
Our blood and water pour from your flowing wounds.
You have cut open our breasts and dug scalpels in our
        brains.
When and Where will another come to take your holy place?
Old man mumbling in his dotage, or crying child, unborn?

# FOR ANDY GOODMAN, MICHAEL SCHWERNER, AND JAMES CHANEY

*Three Civil Rights Workers*
*Murdered in Mississippi on June 21, 1964*
Poem Written After Seeing the Movie, *Andy in A.M.*


Three faces . . .
    mirrored in the muddy stream of living. . . .
young and tender like
quiet beauty of still water,
    sensitive as the mimosa leaf,
    intense as the stalking cougar
    and impassive as the face of rivers;
The sensitive face of Andy
The intense face of Michael
The impassive face of Chaney.

Three leaves . . .
    Floating in the melted snow
    Flooding the Spring
    oak leaves
    one by one
    moving like a barge
    across the seasons
    moving like a breeze across the windowpane
    winter . . . summer . . . spring
When is the evil year of the cricket?
When comes the violent day of the stone?
In which month
do the dead ones appear at the cistern?

Three lives . . .
  turning on the axis of our time
  Black and white together
  turning on the wheeling compass
  of a decade and a day
  The concerns of a century of time
. . . an hourglass of destiny

Three lives . . .
  ripe for immortality of daisies and wheat
  for the simple beauty of a hummingbird
  and dignity of a sequoia
  of renunciation and
  resurrection
For the Easter morning of our Meridians.

Why should another die for me?
Why should there be a calvary
A subterranean hell for three?
In the miry clay?
In the muddy stream?
In the red misery?
In mutilating hatred and in fear?
The brutish and the brazen
without brain
without blessing
without beauty . . .
They have killed these three.
They have killed them for me.

Sunrise and sunset . . .
Spring rain and winter windowpane . . .
I see the first leaves budding
The green Spring returning

I mark the falling
of golden Autumn leaves
and three lives floating down the quiet stream
Till they come to the surging falls. . . .

The burned blossoms of the dogwood tree
tremble in the Mississippi morning
The wild call of the cardinal bird
troubles the Mississippi morning
I hear the morning singing
larks, robins, and the mockingbird
while the mourning dove
broods over the meadow
Summer leaf falls never turning brown

Deep in a Mississippi thicket
I hear that mourning dove
Bird of death singing in the swamp
Leaves of death floating in their watery grave

Three faces turn their ears and eyes
sensitive
intense
impassive
to see the solemn sky of summer
to hear the brooding cry
of the mourning dove

Mississippi bird of sorrow
O mourning bird of death
Sing their sorrow
Mourn their pain
And teach us death,
To love and live with them again!

# PROPHETS FOR A NEW DAY

## I

As the Word came to prophets of old,
As the burning bush spoke to Moses,
And the fiery coals cleansed the lips of Isaiah;
As the wheeling cloud in the sky
Clothed the message of Ezekiel;
So the Word of fire burns today
On the lips of our prophets in an evil age—
Our soothsayers and doom-tellers and doers of the Word.
So the Word of the Lord stirs again
These passionate people toward deliverance.
As Amos, Shepherd of Tekoa, spoke
To the captive children of Judah,
Preaching to the dispossessed and the poor,
So today in the pulpits and the jails,
On the highways and in the byways,
A fearless shepherd speaks at last
To his suffering weary sheep.

## II

So, kneeling by the river bank
Comes the vision to a valley of believers
So in flaming flags of stars in the sky
And in the breaking dawn of a blinding sun
The lamp of truth is lighted in the Temple
And the oil of devotion is burning at midnight
So the glittering censer in the Temple
Trembles in the presence of the priests

And the pillars of the door-posts move
And the incense rises in smoke
And the dark faces of the sufferers
Gleam in the new morning
The complaining faces glow
And the winds of freedom begin to blow
While the Word descends on the waiting World below.


## III


A beast is among us.
His mark is on the land.
His horns and his hands and his lips are gory with our
    blood.
He is War and Famine and Pestilence
He is Death and Destruction and Trouble
And he walks in our houses at noonday
And devours our defenders at midnight.
He is the demon who drives us with whips of fear
And in his cowardice
He cries out against liberty
He cries out against humanity
Against all dignity of green valleys and high hills
Against clean winds blowing through our living;
Against the broken bodies of our brothers.
He has crushed them with a stone.
He drinks our tears for water
And he drinks our blood for wine;
He eats our flesh like a ravenous lion
And he drives us out of the city
To be stabbed on a lonely hill.

# JEREMIAH

Jeremiah, prophet of Jerusalem,
Is now a man whose name is Benjamin
Brooding over a city called Atlanta
Preaching the doom of a curse upon the land;
His native land of Georgia.
Preaching the downfall of an accursed system
Preaching to the righteous of all creeds and colors
And his words are wonderfully wrought
Like the powerful prophets of old:
"Yet I say unto you, verily, not one of these stones shall
        remain.
Not one rock of this rock of hatred shall remain.
This city destroyed by fire a hundred years ago
Rising like a phoenix bird from ashes
To build a mountain of materialism to Mammon
This city must pay and pay and pay
For the horsemen of this city shall be our God's.
My God we are still here. We are still down here Lord,
Working for a Kingdom of Thy Love.
We weep for this city and for this land
We weep for all the doomed people of this land
We weep for Judah and beloved Jerusalem
O Georgia! Where shall you stand in the Judgment?"

# ISAIAH

Isaiah was a man of the court
Who lived in the city and walked with kings;
Isaiah was a cup-bearer for the king.
He was a royal man and he went in and out among the
     people
Speaking his mind to the great.
For the fiery coal on his lips
Was a Word of fire from the Lord.
In the oldest black man's court
With its lawyers and judges and money and men
Sits our northern Isaiah in the City of New York.
There the sorrow of the prophet
Marks his word and his action and his thought
Sorrow sits upon his saddened face and declares his destiny.
In all our seeking after Justice from the law and in the
     Courts
Isaiah is our leader and our man.
And the words of this city-man—this black leader of black
     people—
His words go forth into the world
Carrying to the ends of the earth over waves of light and
     sound
The message of our messenger
Condemning the guilty and the violent
Threatening the complacent
Criticizing the kings seated on thrones
And promising deliverance to a remnant of his people
Isaiah is a city man with a quiet word,
A word of the Lord that demands to be heard.

## AMOS, 1963

Amos is a Shepherd of suffering sheep;
A pastor preaching in the depths of Alabama
Preaching social justice to the Southland
Preaching to the poor a new gospel of love
With the words of a god and the dreams of a man
Amos is our loving Shepherd of the sheep
Crying out to the stricken land
"You have sold the righteous for silver
And the poor for a pair of shoes.
My God is a mighty avenger
And He shall come with His rod in His hand."
Preaching to the persecuted and the disinherited millions
Preaching love and justice to the solid southern land
Amos is a Prophet with a vision of brotherly love
With a vision and a dream of the red hills of Georgia
"When Justice shall roll down like water
And Righteousness like a mighty stream."
Amos is our Shepherd standing in the Shadow of our God
Tending his flocks all over the hills of Albany
And the seething streets of Selma and of bitter Birmingham.

# AMOS (POSTSCRIPT, 1968)

From Montgomery to Memphis he marches
He stands on the threshold of tomorrow
He breaks the bars of iron and they remove the signs
He opens the gates of our prisons.
He speaks to the captive hearts of America
He bares raw their conscience
He is a man of peace for the people
Amos is a Prophet of the Lord
Amos speaks through Eternity
The glorious Word of the Lord!

# JOEL

Joel, that young prophet-son of Pethuel!
Our Joel today, youngest of the young
Standing among the hoary-haired prophets of his people
Joel, young student of the teachers of Truth and
      Righteousness
Joel preaches the wrath and the vengeance of the Lord
Joel preaches the wrath and vengeance of the poor
He cries out against wickedness
He cries out against do-nothingness
Procrastination of people in high places
Of the politicians and the pretenders:
"You have taken my silver and my gold.
You have denied me bread
And cheated my children of the labor of my hands
My God will come and succor all these stricken ones
All his suffering and poor."
Joel is a do-something man
Joel is a young man of action
He is the sit-in suffering without shame
He is the man marching in the streets
And praying on the steps
Filling the jails with song, with singing that is sweet
Joel is the power-wire of living, flaming truth
Joel is the lighted torch of sacrificing youth
Crying, "We shall overcome!"
Crying, "We are not afraid!"
Crying, "We do not fear to die!"
Joel is the torch of truth towering high above the temples
Above the spires and steeples of the synagogues and
      sanctuaries

Lighting the nation with the fire of revelation
Lighting the nation with the everlasting flame of truth
Joel is our burning-hearted youth.
Speak on, Joel, your harsh and bitter words of burning
      Truth.

# HOSEA

Hear this prayer from a Plaquemine jail!
Hear this eloquent, unequivocating cry
From a man the milling mob had marked to die
A man with the love of an Hosea for Gomer
Loving and redeeming a nation's fallen womanhood;
Redeeming lost virtue in the valley of Louisiana
Among the bayous and secretly sinister houses of
    Plaquemine
Redeeming the evil-looking power-masters of a Cult
Of a clique crying out against their Mother Church
Of wolves in sheep's clothing
Scattering the flock, and frightening the lambs
A Plaquemine wolf playing the pipes of a false Pan
From a Plaquemine jail hear the words of Hosea
A prophet not afraid to die
A prophet of love whose love defies
The horses' hooves trampling out the blood of little children
And the cattle prods shocking the squirming flesh with pain
And the firemen's hoses sputtering their hatred
A Prophet in a Plaquemine jail
Sends a letter of love to the world.

# MICAH

*In Memory of Medgar Evers of Mississippi*


Micah was a young man of the people
Who came up from the streets of Mississippi
And cried out his Vision to his people;
Who stood fearless before the waiting throng
Like an astronaut shooting into space.
Micah was a man who spoke against Oppression
Crying: Woe to you Workers of iniquity!
Crying: Woe to you doers of violence!
Crying: Woe to you breakers of the peace!
Crying: Woe to you, my enemy!
For when I fall I shall rise in deathless dedication.
When I stagger under the wound of your paid assassins
I shall be whole again in deathless triumph!
For your rich men are full of violence
And your mayors of your cities speak lies.
They are full of deceit.
We do not fear them.
They shall not enter the City of good-will.
We shall dwell under our own vine and fig tree in peace.
And they shall not be remembered in the Book of Life.
Micah was a man.

# BALLAD OF THE HOPPY-TOAD

Ain't been on Market Street for nothing
With my regular washing load
When the Saturday crowd went stomping
Down the Johnny-jumping road

Seen Sally Jones come running
With a razor at her throat,
Seen Deacon's daughter lurching
Like a drunken alley goat.

But the biggest for my money,
And the saddest for my throw
Was the night I seen the goopher man
Throw dust around my door.

Come sneaking round my doorway
In a stovepipe hat and coat;
Come sneaking round my doorway
To drop the evil note.

I run down to Sis Avery's
And told her what I seen
"Root-worker's out to git me
What you reckon that there mean?"

Sis Avery she done told me,
"Now honey go on back

I knows just what will hex him
And that old goopher sack."


Now I done burned the candles
Till I seen the face of Jim
And I done been to Church and prayed
But can't git rid of him.


Don't want to burn his picture
Don't want to dig his grave
Just want to have my peace of mind
And make that dog behave.


Was running through the fields one day
Sis Avery's chopping corn
Big horse come stomping after me
I knowed then I was gone.


Sis Avery grabbed that horse's mane
And not one minute late
Cause trembling down behind her
I seen my ugly fate.


She hollered to that horse to "Whoa!
I gotcha hoppy-toad."
And yonder come the goopher man
A-running down the road.


She hollered to that horse to "Whoa"
And what you wanta think?

Great-God-a-mighty, that there horse
Begun to sweat and shrink.

He shrunk up to a teeny horse
He shrunk up to a toad
And yonder come the goopher man
Still running down the road.

She hollered to that horse to "Whoa"
She said, "I'm killing him.
Now you just watch this hoppy-toad
And you'll be rid of Jim."

The goopher man was hollering
"Don't kill that hoppy-toad."
Sis Avery she said "Honey,
You bout to lose your load."

That hoppy-toad was dying
Right there in the road
And goopher man was screaming
"Don't kill that hoppy-toad."

The hoppy-toad shook one more time
And then he up and died
Old goopher man fell dying, too.
"O hoppy-toad," he cried.

# ELEGY

*In Memory of Professor Manford Kuhn*

## I

Strange summer sun shines round our globe of
    circumstance.
Light glints on green lives
Like polished leaves on silken surfaces
Washing pavements with widening circles of sunshine
And shadowy patterns laced beneath our feet.
This day a normal time—
Another hour, another year
Of summer fruit and harvest
And of Man.

Cycle of life and Spring of early days
With golden summer ripening into Fall
Winter snow blanketing a slumbering seed
Of new anemone.
Such is life's infancy
And childhood's frothy wood.

## II

Within our house of flesh we weave a web of time
Both warp and woof within the shuttle's clutch
In leisure and in haste no less a tapestry
Rich pattern of our lives.
The gold and scarlet intertwine
Upon our frame of dust an intricate design

Etched solidly by life
In flaming pain and blind
Against the ravages and waste
Of tedium and time,
Until by laughter and the stoic mind
At last the scroll is finished
Then fate unties the knot
And snips the thin-worn twine
With quick release
And quietly we sleep
Marked by an inward peace.

We live again
In children's faces, and the sturdy vine
Of daily influences: the prime
Of teacher, neighbor, student, and friend
All merging on the elusive wind.

# OCTOBER JOURNEY

# OCTOBER JOURNEY

Traveller take heed for journeys undertaken in the dark of
    the year.
Go in the bright blaze of Autumn's equinox.
Carry protection against ravages of a sun-robber, a vandal,
    a thief.
Cross no bright expanse of water in the full of the
    moon.
Choose no dangerous summer nights;
no heavy tempting hours of spring;
October journeys are safest, brightest, and best.


I want to tell you what hills are like in October
when colors gush down mountainsides
and little streams are freighted with a caravan of leaves,
I want to tell you how they blush and turn in fiery shame
    and joy,
how their love burns with flames consuming and terrible
until we wake one morning and woods are like a smoldering
    plain—
a glowing caldron full of jewelled fire;
the emerald earth a dragon's eye
the poplars drenched with yellow light
and dogwoods blazing bloody red.
Travelling southward earth changes from gray rock to green
    velvet.
Earth changes to red clay
with green grass growing brightly
with saffron skies of evening setting dully
with muddy rivers moving sluggishly.

In the early spring when the peach tree blooms
wearing a veil like a lavender haze
and the pear and plum in their bridal hair
gently snow their petals on earth's grassy bosom below
then the soughing breeze is soothing
and the world seems bathed in tenderness,
but in October
blossoms have long since fallen.
A few red apples hang on leafless boughs;
wind whips bushes briskly.
And where a blue stream sings cautiously
a barren land feeds hungrily.

An evil moon bleeds drops of death.
The earth burns brown.
Grass shrivels and dries to a yellowish mass.
Earth wears a dun-colored dress
like an old woman wooing the sun to be her lover,
be her sweetheart and her husband bound in one.
Farmers heap hay in stacks and bind corn in shocks
against the biting breath of frost.

The train wheels hum, "I am going home, I am going home,
I am moving toward the South."
Soon cypress swamps and muskrat marshes
and black fields touched with cotton will appear.
I dream again of my childhood land
of a neighbor's yard with a redbud tree
the smell of pine for turpentine
an Easter dress, a Christmas eve
and winding roads from the top of a hill.
A music sings within my flesh
I feel the pulse within my throat
my heart fills up with hungry fear

while hills and flatlands stark and staring
before my dark eyes sad and haunting
appear and disappear.

Then when I touch this land again
the promise of a sun-lit hour dies.
The greenness of an apple seems
to dry and rot before my eyes.
The sullen winter rains
are tears of grief I cannot shed.
The windless days are static lives.
The clock runs down
timeless and still.
The days and nights turn hours to years
and water in a gutter marks the circle of another world
hating, resentful, and afraid,
stagnant, and green, and full of slimy things.

# HARRIET TUBMAN

Dark is the face of Harriet,
Darker still her fate
Deep in the dark of Southern wilds
Deep in the slaves' hate.

Fiery the eye of Harriet,
Fiery, dark, and wild;
Bitter, bleak, and hopeless
Is the bonded child.

Stand in the fields, Harriet,
Stand alone and still
Stand before the overseer
Mad enough to kill.

This is slavery, Harriet,
Bend beneath the lash;
This is Maryland, Harriet,
Bow to poor white trash.

You're a field hand, Harriet,
Working in the corn;
You're a grubber with the hoe
And a slave child born.

You're just sixteen, Harriet,
And never had a beau;

Your mother's dead long time ago,
Your daddy you don't know.


This piece of iron's not hard enough
To kill you with a blow,
This piece of iron can't hurt you,
Just let you slaves all know.


I'm still the overseer,
Old marster'll believe my tale;
I know that he will keep me
From going to the jail.


Get up, bleeding Harriet,
I didn't hit you hard;
Get up, bleeding Harriet,
And grease your head with lard.


Get up, sullen Harriet,
Get up and bind your head.
Remember this is Maryland
And I can beat you dead.


How far is the road to Canada?
How far do I have to go?
How far is the road from Maryland
And the hatred that I know?


I stabbed that overseer;
I took his rusty knife;

I killed that overseer;
I took his lowdown life.


For three long years I waited,
Three years I kept my hate,
Three years before I killed him,
Three years I had to wait.


Done shook the dust of Maryland
Clean off my weary feet;
I'm on my way to Canada
And Freedom's golden street.


I'm bound to git to Canada
Before another week
I come through swamps and mountains,
I waded many a creek.


Now tell my brothers yonder
That Harriet is free;
Yes, tell my brothers yonder
No more auction block for me.


Come down from the mountain, Harriet,
Come down to the valley at night,
Come down to your weeping people
And be their guiding light.


Sing Deep Dark River of Jordan,
Don't you want to cross over today?

Sing Deep Wide River of Jordan,
Don't you want to walk Freedom's way?


I stole down in the nighttime,
I come back in the day,
I stole back to my Maryland
To guide the slaves away.


I met old marster yonder
A-coming down the road,
And right past me in Maryland
My old marster strode.


I passed beside my marster
And covered up my head;
My marster didn't know me
I guess he heard I'm dead.


I wonder if he thought about
That overseer's dead;
I wondered if he figured out
He ought to know this head?


You'd better run, brave Harriet,
There's ransom on your head;
You better run, Miss Harriet,
They want you live or dead.


Been down in valleys yonder
And searching round the stills,

They got the posse after you,
A-riding through the hills.


They got the bloodhounds smelling,
They got their guns cocked too;
You better run, bold Harriet,
The white man's after you.


They got ten thousand dollars
Put on your coal-black head;
They'll give ten thousand dollars;
They're mad because you fled.


I wager they'll be riding
A long, long time for you.
Yes, Lord, they'll look a long time
Till Judgment Day is due.


I'm Harriet Tubman, people,
I'm Harriet the slave,
I'm Harriet, free woman,
And I'm free within my grave.


Come along, children, with Harriet
Come along, children, come along
Uncle Sam is rich enough
To give you all a farm.


I killed the overseer.
I fooled old marster's eyes,

I found my way to Canada
With hundreds more besides.

Come along to Harpers Ferry
Come along to brave John Brown
Come along with Harriet, children,
Come along ten million strong.

I met the mighty John Brown
I knew Fred Douglass too
Enlisted Abolitionists
Beneath the Union Blue.

I heard the mighty trumpet
That sent the land to war;
I mourned for Mister Lincoln
And saw his funeral car.

Come along with Harriet, children,
Come along to Canada.
Come down to the river, children,
And follow the northern star.

I'm Harriet Tubman, people,
I'm Harriet, the slave,
I'm Harriet, free woman,
And I'm free beyond my grave.

Come along to freedom, children,
Come along ten million strong;
Come along with Harriet, children,
Come along ten million strong.

# EPITAPH FOR MY FATHER

Jamaica is an Island full of Bays
Like jewelled tourmaline set in the sea.
The Caribbean coasts are washed with dazzling sand
So blinding white the sunlight flashes fire,
And trade winds lash against the palm-strewn shore.
Born near Buff Bay my father loved to play
Among the Inlets; shouting over waves
And wading through the sands, would wish to go
Out where the winds would often part the sea,
And as a Hebrew child of long ago
He crossed dry land while waters rose congealed
Till afternoon when once again the winds
Would bring the walls together meltingly
And send the naked children screaming home from play
Or catch the luckless souls upon the open sea.
Those bluest sparkling waters of the Bays—
Montego, Orange, Buff! where many times at play
He watched the ships sail into port of call
And laden with their cargo, their fruit and golden haul
Banana, plantain, palm, palmetto, hemp
Would go again to sea beyond the distances
Where only God knew where, but carefree boys
Would stop their play and longingly gaze far
Out where the ships would disappear from sight
And as the setting sun would light the sky
With flaming rays descending on the sea, as twilight
Travelled from the thin horizon's line
Casting its light to where the mountains stood
Like giants in the Night, dark, high, and still
So homeward they would drag their listless feet

Still thinking of the ships that sailed to foreign shores.
He longed to know the lot of those adventuring
Who join the ocean's fleet and sail into the dusk.
He must have been a very thoughtful lad
Loving his aging mother at her handiwork
Artful with needle and breathing piety,
So full of dreams and ideas for her youngest son.
His father, quite the other sort, could mix
His tavern-keeping with his Lord's day's task at Church
And read the lesson as a layman should.
All his household loved their books;
His brother's full of gibberish and foreign words
Fit for his work, Her Majesty's interpreter
Of all who came from far-off India
Or Germany and France and Spain
And even England's farthest empired land.
And thus this little boy—the last of seven
Would dream of going where the languages
His brother Ben interpreted were known.
But most of all he longed to go to school
In England and at Cambridge, and there
To be a man of learning till once again at home
Where all who knew and loved him would be proud.
Especially his mother, fond and growing old,
But then she died. And he, bereft of all her love,
Disconsolate with grief,
Considered more and more the soonest he could go
Out where the ships plowed through a stormy sea.
My father came to this new land instead,
His dreams of Cambridge roughly put aside
Where opportunity and expediency
A round-about long journey carried him
Before he touched the soil at Mobile Bay.
But still he hoped to study, then return

To make his mark at home; his papers drawn
Allowed him only rights of visitors, a visa
Stated when he hoped to finish here.
He never left. When all the scholar's honors he could heap
Into a pile were won, he saw my mother's face
And turned aside briefly to gaze
Upon the aura, charm and grace
In which she spoke and smiled and played—
Her fingers dancing over ivoried keys.
So they were wed, his child-bride all too young
From Pensacola's Bay dashed starry-eyed away
With this strange son come from a foreign land—
An older sadder soul, ambitious, proud and quite removed
From life's realities and practicalities;
A dreamer, quiet, seriously withdrawn
From enmities and hates, yet hurt by them
And startled by the strange ironic turn
Of epithets: "You, monkey-chaser, You nigger, You, I mean!"
And thus they came to live in Birmingham.
When I was very young and still quite small
My father used to take me on his knee
And say to me, "My little one, I wish that you could see
The land where I was born—so beautiful!
With fruit so sweet and land so rich
Where black men, too, are free.
Star apples and breadfruit trees
The mangoes and the coconuts
Date palms and yams and green banana trees
Cassava, pumpkins, okra too
Just like the okra here and alligator pear
And flowers, oh, the blossoms there
That grow so wild and so profuse
And every color of the rainbow only brighter
And bolder and richer in their hue

More blue, more red, more orange than the rind
Of melons that we grow
And black men, too, live side by side
With yellow, white, and brown
And they have not this craziness
Of jim crow and race prejudice.
I never thought this place could be so full of bitterness."
And yet he never went back again
He took his papers out to be a citizen
Yet all his life he talked about his home
And going to that Island in the sea.
When I was five his father died
And there was no one left
To take him back. The final tie was gone.
I saw the letter and his unshed tears.
The earliest memories I have
Are seeing all my father's hours spent in toil
From teaching daily, preaching Sundays
Tailoring at night to give us bread.
In summer, wintertime and fall
His days were all the same—
No time in fun. Relaxing by the fire
He fell asleep and snored
And mama cried annoyed, "Get up and go to bed!"
And in the night how often could I hear
Both whispering of future plans for us,
For buying shoes and clothes and sending us to school
Always to keep a roof above our heads
And sometimes I would hear my father say,
"Let's buy a car!" And mama said:
"We can't afford it now."
Or else he'd want a bigger house with stairs
And mama horrified would cry, "Not now."
He would buy her pretty dresses

And say, "Surprise!" and she would say
"I have to hold your father down."
"He thinks that all his family should dress in golden wings."
I liked it when my father went to town
And bought our clothes
No hand-me-downs made-over things,
He bought the best and struggled hard to pay,
And tried to keep in check his great desire for books.
Two times we moved from Birmingham.
The first to Haven in Meridian and back again.
And then to New Orleans. At first my mother was a wraith,
A frail and walking ghost with babies in her arms
And many nights I dreamed that she would die
And dying passed beside my bed.
I screamed to wake her, went to touch her arm,
Sometimes not sure, would crawl beside her
Feeling safer there.
But time relentlessly moved on the years
And from the twilight time
When first I saw her bending down
Above her dying sister's bed
And daddy writing, "Please come home again
Everything here is going to Fillymanew."
And on the train that carried us away from home and
        friends
Till past the blue dim past of years in New Orleans
And Mardi Gras with nights of bitter cold
When Daddy took us out to see parades;
My father's summers off at summer school
And figs and biscuits and water were all we had to eat;
Until my graduation days.
Then off at college hearing ominous reports
Depression and no salary checks at home
And letters from my mother, "Don't do this or that.

Wear your green dress. Don't sit up late.
Stay off Chicago streets at night."
My father seemed so far away; his letters seldom;
Yet when I read the few lines many times
I thought with pride, how well he writes!
But conversations late at night with him
Were best, for now he ventured out
And said what reading I should do for depth.
His favorites were mine: the Greeks and Romans
And from the Bible all the words of Paul;
The Sage of Königsberg;
The gentle Spinoza;
Fichte and Schopenhauer;
Whitehead, the English classics;
Poetry and mystics and the wine of all the ancient East:
Buddha, Confucius, Lao-tse, "The Gita," then Gandhi's
        way;
And when he said, "I wish your verse were more religious,"
I pertly said, "It can't be what I'm not!"
And wished I'd cut my tongue out; only then
My lips were always in a pout rebelliously.
If I had been a man
I might have followed in his every step,
Had preached from pulpits, found my life as his
And wandered too, as he, an alien on the earth,
But female and feline I could not stand
Alone through love and hate and truth
And still remain my own. He was himself;
His own man all his life.
And I belong to all the people I have met,
Am part of them, am molded by the throng
Caught in the tide of compromise, and grown
Chameleon for camouflage. Yet I have known
A noble princelike man for all my life,

For he was humble in his dignity
Composed and calm in every storm of life,
Harsh poverty could not debase, demean
His deep integrity. He rose above the fray.
And when at last my children came
His joy was indescribable:
"I only wish they had not come so late in life for me."
Now travelling everywhere about this land
The golden years descended on his head,
And with my mother he saw the promised land
Of California, Boston, and New York,
Nebraska, Philadelphia, and then
When suddenly the shades of night began to fall
The ship at sea was tossed and buffeted
He stood and watched the light
That beckons every pilot to his harbor's home
In resignation to the will and fate
Of Providence, the destiny of Men.
In dreams I stood beside him, heard him say
"I came to tell you I'm about to go away.
I'm going to a church meeting, very great.
My name is on the program, I want to look my best."
And pointed to the undertaker's suit;
I begged him not to go, but then he smiled
"Child, don't you understand? I'm going to be promoted!"
And sadly waved at me.
That day I sat as in a dream and heard
The preacher echoing familiar words:
"We spend our years as a tale that is told;
The days of our years are three-score years and ten."
I glanced through windows, saw the sun
Peep from the clouds in one bright blaze of gold
Lighting the casket where he lay so cold
And then I knew that he would never die—

Not on the earth or in the sky or sea.
He did not leave a fortune made with gold
Nor lands and wealth of human hands
But all the deep recesses of our minds and hearts
Were filled with plunder from the Ages old:
The way to greet a stranger and a guest;
The love to bear a friend and how to pray
In deep compassion for an enemy;
The courage and the faith to face all life;
The willingness to learn new lessons every day;
Humility and truth and deep integrity—
This is the Epitaph that I would write for him.

# ODE ON THE OCCASION
# OF THE INAUGURATION
# OF THE SIXTH PRESIDENT OF
# JACKSON STATE COLLEGE

I

Give me again the flaming torch of truth
that burned before the altars of our gods;
the spirit nascent, sleeping on the breasts
of black men born to die on foreign shores
on battlefields, and on familiar trees
hanging with bloody forms and blackened bones
kindled to death by lynching mobs.
I burn to bring you words from oracles
from temple fires and smoking flambeaux
snatched from hands of running warriors;
to speak the fiery words of bronzed and sepia men
whose broken threads of time
were cut before their prime
the primitive and halcyon days
before the shame of slave ships brought black men here
to sacred lands of red men
and changed them into whitened sepulchres of hate.
Dark were the years
that spawned three centuries of toil and trouble
deep in this southern land
before our fathers heard of liberty
and learned that freedom did not come
when chains of bondage fell from shackled limbs
and not from minds and hearts

still chained in ignorance,
and circumscribed by prejudice and hate.
For days like these we need the truth.
We need the shower-washing deluging of truth.
Beneath the slavers' rod
chastisement of the soul
the brutal lashing of the mind
the whip of ignorance.
Broken but not demented by the charge
of mental shock and cruelty.
Offended by outrage
but never blown apart by bitterness.

Record the day when millions of our kin went free
to wander homeless in a devastated land
against the hostile wrath of brutish men
sullen and sulking in defeat
yet mired themselves in darkest ignorance.
Was it the dove of peace
bearing the twig of olive in her beak
that wrought a miracle?
Or was it phoenix bird of poetry
Winged Pegasus that lifted high the dream
to mountain height and bade the black and unknown bards
express their longing for the truth?
Perhaps, instead the eagle eye
of money and greed for gold and land
lifted her face first to freedom's hallowed light
while Justice, blind, was balancing the scales
and Truth was bleeding on a cross of shame.
This place of learning came instead
from humble men,
and Education shone its rays upon
weak vessels of the Lord

born in a House of Prayer
and in the consciences of Christian hearts
this place we call a College was first conceived.


**II**


Up from the Mississippi soil
her sons and daughters came
from red-clay hills and delta land
the coastal plains
from barren rocks, from loam and sand
they came with hunger for the truth
for knowledge and the need to understand
the meaning of our living in this southern land.
And so he came
fresh from the war
a war fought, too, for liberty
as all wars, so they say, are fought
and like all black men living in America
he came without the heroes' welcoming
as all black men returning home from foreign wars
to make the world safe for democracy
to end all wars
to give us freedom, life, and liberty
as all black men
have found the hope of truth
turn ashes in the mouth.
And like his people
symbols of the land
he found the high tides of his destiny
our destiny, one people and one man
who seek a free and noble land
a nation high with destiny, with promise unfulfilled

a race of men who can
yet make the dream come true
now in this time of truth
a people hearing universally
a Cry for freedom ringing in this land
The hands of destiny now mark this clock of life
and after time, a hundred years now passed
searching for freedom is our destiny
that all men everywhere may see
the blinding face of truth
and thus may know
and knowing may be forever free.


## III


O bird of paradise,
bird of wilderness
cardinal bird of truth
now sing the song I long to sing
the song of hope and love
pride in our past
faith for our future
and hope undimmed by all our ancient fears,
Sing now a paean for this man
a prayer breathed on the wings
of shifting winds
that search the world
and bring the storm of change into our land.
Now steady one man's hand
and may the winds of fate
be neither harsh nor rude.
Sing birds of paradise,
bird of the wilderness, now sing!

# DEAR ARE THE NAMES
# THAT CHARMED ME
# IN MY YOUTH

DEAR are the names that charmed me in my youth:
    the dark bronze faces I rejoiced to see.
One taught me love, another taught me truth
and one of them brought bitterness and ruth.
But all of them inspired my life to be
a charging promise ringed with rhapsody.

Now once again I lift my eyes to them:
who now would make my life a purpose-tree
on which I strive to climb from limb to limb
up where my challenges may rise defiantly.

I cannot blame another for my fate
nor cry a cropper full of tears and glee.
Why should I burgeon memories with hate?
I have no right, and no necessity.

# I WANT TO WRITE

I want to write
I want to write the songs of my people.
I want to hear them singing melodies in the dark.
I want to catch the last floating strains from their sob-torn
    throats.
I want to frame their dreams into words; their souls into
    notes.
I want to catch their sunshine laughter in a bowl;
fling dark hands to a darker sky
and fill them full of stars
then crush and mix such lights till they become
a mirrored pool of brilliance in the dawn.

# FOR GWEN, 1969

*Gwendolyn Brooks*


The slender, shy, and sensitive young girl
is woman now,
her words a power in the Ebon land.
Outside her window on the street
a mass of life moves by.
Chicago is her city.
Her heart flowers with its flame—
old stockyards, new beaches
all the little storefront churches
and the bar on the corner.
Dreamer and seer of tales
She witnesses rebellion,
struggle and sweat.
The people are her heartbeat—
In their footsteps pulsate daily
all her black words of fire and blood.

# FOR PAUL LAURENCE DUNBAR

*Centennial Celebration, Dayton, Ohio, 1972*


A man whose life was like a candle's flame:
faint, flickering, and brightened with the poet's light.
He came to earth a butterfly of time
and lifted in his hands the spirit-dust;
gave to the world chameleon his singing heart
and sacrificed upon the altar fame
his glowing candle fire of life and love.

Remembering, we pause to honor him
but knowing well the Ages honor best
his image, frail and pure, while millions here
behold his comet-star and see its flaming trail
burst brilliantly across the burning sky.
We hold aloft his laughter-breaking, black,
and bitter songs, and his immortal name.

# FOR MARY McLEOD BETHUNE

Great Amazon of God behold your bread
Washed home again from many distant seas
The cup of life you lift contains no lees
No bitterness to mock you, in its stead
So many, gone this brimming chalice fed
And broken-hearted people on their knees
Look up to you and suddenly they seize
On living faith and they are comforted.
Believing in the people who are free
Who walk uplifted in an honest way
You look at last upon another day
That you have fought with God and man to see.
Great Amazon of God behold your bread,
We walk with you, and we are comforted.

# TRIBUTE TO ROBERT HAYDEN

*February, 1980*


For this man
I first read
forty years ago.
Quiet, bespectacled
Loving music and religion—
Loving God and mankind—
Speaking pearls and weaving
tapestries—
Drinking from fountains of
wisdom, truth and beauty
Teaching us Divinity.
I think across the years—
young man of twenty-two
writing *Heart Shape in the Dust*
years in Nashville
years eaten by the locusts
1952 and Jackson State College
Seventy-fifth Anniversary
with Langston and Arna
and Owen and Melvin Tolson
Sterling and me—
A happy time.

Twenty years later
again in the same place
sadder, wiser, softer
More profound
across the years
a multiplicity of Jewelled words

taken from the casket of memory
like a magician with legerdemain.
Meanwhile, New York and Washington
The velvet canopy
The cloth of gold
The African legend and the world prize
and always too
Irma spelling music
making the spell with music
Moving into mystical realms
of life eternally good.

"Runnagate—runnagate
mean mean to be free"

*Kaleidoscope*
all the books
all the years
all the songs
still shining in our ears

O master fabricator
make us another shining song.

# FOR OWEN DODSON, 1983

And will they weep for us
As we do now for you
Drink all our tears
And emptying each cup
Turn more up
For the waiting taste
Of wine, of life,
Of all our little fears?—


Oh brother gone into the night
Against the raging wind
And tempest-tossed seas
If only for a little while
Look back
Give up your laughing eyes
Your elfin face
And pity us
Left here to grief and windless sighs
I see him now across these
Forty years—
Striding over Hampton's green
A few years later in
New Orleans
With a Guggenheim and off to
Write in Italy
Those two wonderful weeks
In Jackson, Mississippi 1952
Langston, Arna, Sterling, Tolson,
Bob Hayden and Owen all were here

Owen brought his Devine Comedy
To us and Carolyn
Mr. Peterson was Father Devine
I saw him next in Washington at Howard
1977 Owen came again to Jackson
This time on crutches
And that last time in New York
In his penthouse
Seeing Edith there
Over the telephone we talked about
Dick Wright and letters
And my last conversation with him
Over the telephone in April
Only two months ago
Now he is gone—
Saddened, shocked and stunned
But only for one brief hour
Of tears and rain
I will remember the sun
Sunshine and blue skies
And laughter against the pain.
His spirit now has wings
No longer fettered
He was born to be free.
And now he has no shackles
He goes free.

Did Edith beckon to you
From the top of a distant hill?
Did she come calling in the night
To lead you through the seas
Or cross you over on the other side?

Dear Owen—brother of our brightest years
        So brilliant, beautiful, and brave—
        Sleep now—the furies disappear
        The demons ride the wind
        And you are always here.

# BALLAD FOR PHILLIS WHEATLEY

*Written for the Bicentennial Celebration of the Publication of Phillis Wheatley's* Poems on Various Subjects, Religious and Moral, *1773*

Pretty little black girl
standing on the block,
how have you withstood this shame,
bearing all this shock?

How have you succeeded
weathering the trip?
How have you come through the stench,
riding on this stinking ship?

Pretty little black girl,
come, go home with me.
I will take you far away
from this painful sea.

This is little Phillis
shedding two front teeth.
This is little Phillis,
caught and torn beneath

all the bright blue canopy
of her native land;
caught and kidnapped far away
from her native land.

Child bereft of mother,
father stricken so;

"What will happen to our little one?
 Who will see her grow?"

"Boston is a cold town
 Ice, and snow, and rain.
 Nothing like a tropic world,
 nothing like the Plain

 I have known in Africa:
 warm and soft and green.
 I am sick for Africa;
 take me home again!

 And I think I cannot bear
 all the anguish here:
 faces pale and men with whips,
 danger always near."

 Pretty little black girl
 no one now can see
 all the greatness you will know,
 all that you will be.

 Pretty little black girl
 standing on the block
 how have you withstood this shame,
 bearing all this shock?

# A LITANY

# FROM THE DARK PEOPLE

From ignorance and darkness, stupidity, and fears;
From chains of chattel slavery, and sullen evil years;
From hopelessness, and helplessness, and brokenhearted
    tears;
From desperate miasma of floundering under jeers;
From stooping to the Sunday-folks and bending to the lash;
From weeping over children lost, the desperate and the
    rash;
From shuddering and shivering upon the auction stand;
From walking in the shackled line and dying hand in hand;
From bleeding in the battlelines and fighting in the fields;
From slipping through the canebrake to the pittance sorrow
    yields;

        O God of earth and sky and sea,
        Great God of love and majesty,
        Thine humble servants everyone
        In mercy have we come.

From dreaming of the golden harps to play upon and sing;
From sitting at the welcome board where milk and honey
    spring;
From wearing of that long white robe with sandals on our
    feet;
From talking with our Jesus-King where peace and glory
    meet;
From climbing Jacob's ladder and wrestling till the day;
From riding in a chariot up where the angels play;
From laying down our sword and shield down by the
    riverside

And walking up the glory-road with Jesus at our side;
From ringing of the golden bells and touching gates of pearl;
From turning backs to sorrow and the evil sin-washed world;

> O God of earth and sky and sea,
> Great God of love and majesty,
> Thine humble servants everyone
> In mercy have we come.

From planting of the cotton crop and bending with the hoe;
From pulling the tobacco plants across each wearying row;
From hovels in the backwoods and cabins by the sea;
From crying after happiness and craving to be free;
From weeping in the nighttime and shouting in the day;
From wombs of bitter penury we've found our lowly way
Up from the night of slavery and persecution's thrall;
Up from the soil of wasted hopes where bitter teardrops fall;
Up from the deepest dungeon and from the darkest night;
Into the day of learning and of Education's light;

> O God of earth and sky and sea,
> Great God of love and majesty,
> Thine humble servants everyone
> By mercy have we come.

From grasping of the helping hand the whiter brother cast;
With golden guineas handed down to end the shameful past;
From building empires of our own with brain and brawn
    and prayers;
From working to enlarge the gift of him who gladly shares;
From lifting fallen brothers and rising as we climb
To build a race of leaders and a nation more sublime;
From giving our talents in measures full and free
To speed the coming of that day when all mankind shall be

United under God in love and charity
And Thy Kingdom shall abide on earth through all eternity;

O God of earth and sky and sea,
Great God of love and majesty,
Thine humble servants everyone
In mercy have we come.

# THIS IS
# MY CENTURY

# THIS IS MY CENTURY

## Black Synthesis of Time

**I**

O Man, behold your destiny.
Look on this life
and know our future living;
our former lives from these our present days
now melded into one.

Queens of the Nile,
Gods of our Genesis,
Parade of centuries
behold the rising sun.
The dying Western sky
with yawning gates of death,
from decadence and dissonance
destroying false and fair;
worlds of our galaxies,
our waning moons and suns
look on this living hell
and see the rising sun.

**II**

Speak, heralds of our honored dead
Proclaim the heroes' line.
Declaim the sculptured and created truths
from prehistoric time.

Infinitude is bared to finite eyes:
We see the whirling suns and stars
first fixed and moving space
to shape beginning Time.


## III

This is my century
I saw it grow
from darkness into dawn.
I watched the molten lava pour
from red volcanic skies;
Islands and Mountains heave
into the Sea
Move Man into the spiralled axis turn
and saw six suns and sunsets rise and burn.


## IV

Osiris, Isis, black and beauteous gods,
whence came your spectacle
of rhythmed life and death?
You gods of love
on pyres of sacrifice
our human hearts become
old hearthstones of our tribal birth and flame:
the hammer and the forge,
the anvil and the fire,
the righteous sparks go wild
like rockets in the sky.
The fireworks overhead
flame red and blue and gold

against one darkened sky.
O living man behold
your destined hands control
the flowered earth ablaze,
alive, each golden flower unfold.


Now see our marching dead
The tyrants too, have fled.
The broken bones and blood
Have melted in the flood.


## V  Cinque (From the Amistad)


Cinque.
O man magnificent.
The gods endowed you well.
Prince of our innocence
the stars move round your head.
You stride the earth to tell
your sons and daughters young
from island, sea, and land—
a continental span—
how men are made of gods
and born to rule the world.
In majesty with monumental hands
you bridge the Universe
and centuries of desert sands.
Bequeath to us your handsome dignity
and lordly noble trust.

## VI

Gods of compassion, rise
In mortal human form.
The splendor of your eyes
Streaks lightning through the storm.

## VII

This is my century—
Black synthesis of Time:
The freudian slip
The Marxian mind
Kierkegaardian Leap of Faith
and Du Bois' prophecy: the color line.
These are the comrades of Einstein,
the dawning of another Age,
new symphony of Time.

## VIII

New liberties arise;
from Freedom's flag unfold;
the right to live and be
both stronger and more wise.
Each child, a prophet's eyes;
each place, a priestess stone.
This Beast no man denies
the godly-human throne.
Each generation cries
to touch divinity
and open up the sunlit splitting skies.

# IX

I have had a good time singing
the songs of my fathers
the melodies of my mothers
the plaintive minor notes of my grandmothers.
I heard the drums of Africa
and I made the music of Spain.
I gave rhythm to the world
and called it syncopation.
All the Calypso brothers
have danced music in my head
and all my beautiful jazzy greats
like old Satchmo,
the Duke, the Count, the Duchess, the King
the Queen, Prince, and Princesses
they were the sons and daughters of royalty
in my dynasty.
I am a black shoeshine boy
made immortal by Barthe'
and I am a black mother
running from slavery.

# X

Look on my bronzed and black-red-mahogany face
and know me well.
For I am the seed of the earth,
the broken body of the Son of God,
and the Spirit of the Universe.
Drink wine in my memory
and pour water on stones
singing Libation songs.

I came out of the sun
and I swam rivers of blood
to touch the moon.
I will not flinch before the holocaust
for I am a deathless soul,
immortal, black, and free.

# GIANTS OF MY CENTURY

Five men shaped this century
with their thinking, breathing, loving lives.
They measured out the land of all our years
and blew the trumpets of the decades in our ears.

## I  Albert Einstein

A hundred years ago was born a man
whose vision of the universe exceeded space and time
beyond the measuring of finite spheres
into illimitable, vast, and recreating galaxies of stars.
He wrote the bars
of music
formulated dreams
and three equations of the nuclear Age.
A face of innocence, a brain of ancient tense,
a catalyst and maker of the Age.
His theories sounded vaguely in our minds
of finite and the infinite, of relativity;
the unity of time and knowledge and diversity
the waves of light and energy and space continuum with
        time.
A hundred years ago just such a man was born.

## II  Sigmund Freud

The Freudian Age has covered, too, our time
within this century.

One Sigmund Freud, a prophet born in ancient times
like all the others from despised sons
and all but one, a Jew
not of the Aryan Race but Wizardry.
His is the stuff of which our sleep and dreams are made.
Psychoanalysis
into the Ego, Id, Libido
and deep analysis into subconsciousness.
Sex is the key?
At least one key for males,
if *not* for me.


## III  Karl Marx


Marx is the man for whom the revolutions come and go.
Not Austria-Prussia;
strangely Germany was not the first
But Russia: Lenin, Trotsky were the first to burst
the hammer and the sickle and their flag of blood
against the northern, polar sky.
And yet his dreaming rages on
across a century
through fire and blood and agony
on every continent but one and in each hemisphere
the revolutions come and go.
This madness rages on
to make the workers free?
to lift the lowest down
divide the wealth and land
and live communally?

## IV  Søren Kierkegaard

Kierkegaard—a lonely tragic man
whose leap of faith gives hope
to those believers who believing Can
and thus believing leave despair and dread,
the sickness unto death;
discover purity
and know one Will to Will.
We know at last the differences
between the will to Be
and merely to exist.
Of alienation too, beyond the pale
of neighbor, race, and clan
to be alone, outside, and yet to Be.
Thus was his destiny and life—
this lonely, tragic, man.


## V  William Edward Burghardt Du Bois

Du Bois, I know you well;
Brother of my flesh, my kith and kin;
Race of my Race, man of Humanity.
They could not hope to know
how seminal your mind was for us all;
the seeds of truth, of destiny, and love
were sown by you; your broken dreams
evolving ever higher into realms
beyond the earth and sea into a land
where we are gods and touch divinity.

Make me a monument for five men:
Marx and Freud

Einstein, Du Bois, Kierkegaard
and build no more.
They have their feet upon the floor
of ocean sand
and their heads are above clouds.
They are the giants of my century.
Their words are prophesies
lighting our decades.
Their smiles are rainbows
arching the planet's globe.
When they sing
cadences of love songs and music of machines
lullabies in the night
break our dread existence into luminous day.
These are the men who marshalled aeons of satellites;
planetary stars and galaxies yet unborn.
These are the doctors, nurses, midwives ushering our birth.
Our umbilical cord
is wasted in the vapid dawn
of prehistoric time
hidden in caves of gargantuan mists.
And they were there.

# FIVE BLACK MEN...

## And ten will save the city.

Douglass, Du Bois, Garvey, King, and Malcolm X
Five black men whose leadership we cherish
in the history books
from Slavery to Segregation and the Age of Integration
down the primrose path to face oblivion

Five Black Men . . .
*and ten will save the city.*

Douglass was the first
brooding face upon our dark waters
rising out of twilight
clutching stars
daring the sun
casting light from all ages
on our miserable circumstance.

Yes, we know our black brothers in Africa
sold their mothers and sisters into slavery.
Yes, we know our white brothers in Europe
packed us like sardines in cans on their stinking ships
and we died like flies.

"I have known the curse of slavery
and the master's cruel will
the overseer's lash and the reveille at dawn;
when the freedom talkers came
they called my name
but I was not on the roll of the chained

nor the dead
lying before the merciless pity of the yankees.
I was long since gone.
Lincoln and Garrison
John Brown and the Alcotts
they were all the same—
aflame with one true mockery
of freedom, truth, and faith
but not for brotherhood.
I tell you my fellow shackled human race
we must strike the first blow.
We must be free
by the blood of our own humanity."

Five Black Men . . .
          *and ten will save the city.*

Du Bois was Renaissance. . .
Ancient Egypt, Thebes, and Memphis
Cush and Temples of Karnak, Luxor, and Parthenon
They were his temples too.
He stood astride the chasm of yawning worlds
bridging the centuries
holding bolts of lightning
electric in his fist.
First social doctor of our century
analyzing our lives, our cities, our towns and schools;
loving our people
and understanding
how western man built his system
on the labor of our lives
cheap labor, slave labor, from dusk till dawn;
how they made a myth out of race
joined it to their christianity

and annihilated our lives.
Du Bois reminded us and prophesied:
"The problem of the twentieth century will be the color
        line."

Five Black Men . . .
        *and ten will save the city.*

Marcus Garvey.
Up, you mighty Race!
And clench your fist against the sky.
Black is beautiful.
Say it loud, I'm black and I'm proud.
Visionary, man of destiny,
Black Messiah?
The United Negro Improvement Association lives.
The black star ascends.
The black ships and black cross nurses
all are part of a lost black empire.
They followed Garvey from the grass roots
by the tens, by the hundreds,
and then by the thousands;
marched down Lenox Avenue in New York
And State Street in Chicago.
Then the mighty ones saw his power.
Was he really guilty of mail fraud
or was that a way the GI guys could stop him?
A way to make him rot in jail in Atlanta
in the U.S.A.

Discredited, denounced, deported,
but not destroyed.
First black nationalist of this century;
Big Black Man, you were never small.

You gave black men hope and dignity and Face.
Up, I say, Up, you might Race!

Five Black Men . . .
*and ten will save the city.*

"The King is Dead. Long live the King!"
He gave us more than life.
"If they ask you why he came
tell them he came
to wake the conscienceless. . . .
tell them he came
to teach us how to dream."*

Atlanta born
Educated there and in Boston
Pastor of Dexter Street Baptist Church
Downtown in Montgomery
He led us through the bloody streets of Birmingham
We walked and talked with him
in Mississippi and Iowa
in Cicero and Harlem
Our hearts followed him to Oslo
And we held our breath
to see his meteor in the sky
Shocked by the assassin's rifle in Memphis
we sorrowed and we spoke
same gun that killed Medgar
same gun that killed Kennedy
same gun.
The king is dead. Long live the king!
A man of peace is immortal
beyond the price of segregation.

*Kelly Miller Smith

Five Black Men . . .
        *and ten will save the city.*

The old man had the message.
The old man never went to school
but he sent his sons.
The old man knew the depth of hatred
between the races
and he knew the history of hatred
between Jew and Christian and Moslem.
He preached his message from Allah
The message he received from Mr. Fard.
I remember those early days
when the brothers of Mecca
wore red fezzes
dressed neatly
and walked circumspectly
in our neighborhoods.
I remember when children turned their heads
curiously to see
why they looked so different
so strange among us
and yet were black like us.
Tell me now the old man amassed a fortune
Tell me now the old man had his lieutenant killed.
Tell me now the brothers killed Malcolm.
And I cannot believe you.
Nothing inside my gut reaction tells me this is true.

Malcolm, the man
Big Cat
was feline in his grace;
leonine head
and cat eyes

and hair to match his lion's sign:
Big Red

Only when he lay dead
and in his funeral moslem dress
did we cast Christian eyes of wonder upon him.
"Ye shall know a tree by the fruit it bears."
too late to know
how measureless for all time was this man.

Five Black Men . . .
   *and ten will save the city.*

Martin and Malcolm
were leaders of men.
They made revolutions.
They fought wars.
They drew battlelines
and never once
with loaded guns.
Their words were their weapons.
Their deeds were their monuments.
No two men more unlike
yet in all that matters they were the same.
In one bright, hopeless, fated Cause
they were brothers.

Five Black Men . . .
   *and ten will save the city.*

# ON DEATH
# AND THE RESURRECTION

I am Osiris
Spirit of the Nile, God of the Dead,
and ruler of the nether regions.
In all the underworld
I am the Lord of passage
from death to life eternal.
Within the Hall of Justice
Before the Throne of Righteousness
Across the black waters
I am the captain of the ship,
the ferryman, the holder of the helm,
the charioteer.
And you will find me seated
before the doors of all the royal tombs
wherein these dead have taken up their long abode
and here have brought their household goods
their servants and their kin
their precious gems and food, water, corn, and grain
and all their furnishings to make them comfortable.
I am Osiris,
Lord of the Dead, and Prince of the Resurrection.

# MY MISSISSIPPI SPRING

My heart warms under snow;
flowers with forsythia,
japonica blooms, flowering quince,
bridal wreath, blood root and violet;
yellow running jasmin vine,
cape jessamine and saucer magnolias:
tulip-shaped, scenting lemon musk upon the air.
My Mississippi Spring—
my warm loving heart a-fire
with early greening leaves,
dogwood branches laced against the sky;
wild forest nature paths
heralding Resurrection
over and over again
Easter morning of our living
every Mississippi Spring!

# BLACK PARAMOUR

I am the woman of kings;
the love supreme of emperors;
of ancient Nubian conquerors,
and men of destiny.
I couched with the Borgias and the Caesars,
with Claudius and Antony,
and I knew Rimini.
I was with the Bourbons
and I colored the pages of all the tedious stages
in History. Poets and composers
worshipped at my shrine.
I nourished them with nectar and with wine,
ambrosia of the gods.
Lust for power, wealth, and fame
pulsed through their sensual veins,
while music, art, and poetry, and sculptured stone
thrived round my purple throne.
I was the fate of Empires lost
when kingdoms crumbled into dust.
My hate drew dire revenge and vengeance from on high;
your late Olympus heard my cry
and Eros, Bacchus, Venus all enraged
Black Isis, Astoreth, Astarte, all upstaged
invoked their Ares-Mars for war.
Cupidity and their vulgarity
brought evil to my side
and in those days of danger made me ride
far from the death of love and dreams
to find another light-of-love
and still a regal queen

today, I quickly leave the scene
before they know the deadly role I play:
the asp upon my bosom, the poison on my tongue;
how much my sexual royalty has wrung
and what by politic I mean;
what storms my slaves of passion stirred,
how much because of me occurred,
nor let them now forget they knew my dust
forgetting all their vampire lust
while I remain eternally the same—
Black paramour, eternal vestal flame.

# A LITANY OF BLACK HISTORY
# FOR BLACK PEOPLE

Leader:   For all our noble heritage:
The brave enduring men;
For those whose hands upheld them,
Courageous now as then:
The women who were mothers,
The wives and barren kin;
For all who laid the bottom rung
Who succored foe and friend;
For those who fell beneath the lash
Who died choked in the chain,
Whose broken bodies fed the birds
Whose only sons were slain
In war and pestilence, in mobs,
In riots, and on trees,
Burned thousands caught beneath the floods,
Who died within the dream—

Chorus:   Thanks be to God in all our love
For brave humanity
We lift our hearts in gratitude
We hail this century.

Leader:   For youth who dared defy us
To fight for liberty
Who willingly would rather die
Than live and not be free;
For children who were willing
To sacrifice their all
And die in streets,

Be bombed in church
And face the maddened dogs;
Who broke the chains
Swift forged again
Who *sat* away the signs
That separated man from man
And broke the laws of God.

Chorus:   Thanks be to God and all our hope
For all humanity
We lift our hands in gratitude
We take this century.

Leader:   Beyond the years of suffering
Adversity and tears
Beyond the penuries of life
Of slavery and fears
Beyond the alabaster gates
Of cities through the veil
Beyond the mockery of fate
The bitter dark travail
Against the walls of stony pride
Against the living hell
On shining hills before us
The light of life prevails.

Chorus:   Thanks be to God and all our love
For great humanity
We stand today in gratitude
We own this century.

Leader:   For sons and daughters yet unborn
Who own the future years
Humanity and in all its pride

Full grown, divine, and free
Who look beyond the outer rim
Of deathless, fearless dreams
And see the gods we dare become
And see God's kingdom here;
For race-less men whose faces burn
With light of love and peace
Whose understanding goes beyond
Wide realms of outer reach
Whose footsteps echo bells of home
We lift our blinded sight.

Chorus:    Thanks be to God, our sacred faith
Has brought us through the years
In humble loyalty we rise
We claim this century!

# ON YOUTH AND AGE

**I**

The year I was born was a nodal year;
Fifty years since black chattel slavery
World War I was just beginning,
One quarter million black people left Mississippi.
That was the year Carter G. Woodson
began to celebrate Black History Week.
Another man in the White House was ending
his presidential term.

I saw President Harding when I was eight.
White haired white man in a white suit
riding in a white limousine in Birmingham.
And we thought he was wonderful
'cause he waved to us black children
on one side of the street
just like he waved to the white children
on the other side of the street.
I saw him with my own eyes.

**II**

I was twelve when Lindbergh crossed the ocean;
Thirty-eight hours in the 'Spirit of St. Louis';
That tall blond nordic hero of the West
with blue eyes piercing through the dawn
wearing goggles
flying a crate nobody would cross the street today.

They brought him home to a ticker-tape parade
with millions screaming and churning confetti
from Wall Street. . . .
two years before the stockmarket crashed. . . .
five years later in the news again
with a baby boy kidnapped
and a German criminal blamed.

Did the black man ever get the reward money?
There were no black servants
Like the Irish Kennedys who said they knew no Negroes.
Like the year of the Watergate
when the black hero lost his job and couldn't find another
while the criminals lived up their millions in luxury.
They even accused Mr. Lindbergh of being a Nazi
before it was all over.
But the trans-Atlantic flights have never stopped
even when Amelia Earhart went down
somewhere out there over the Pacific.
Disasters continue to spread through the air like disease.
The airplane came to stay for a century.

The Age of Aviation became the Jet Age,
And this, too, is my century.


III


When I was a little girl
the little girl on Morton Salt was white;
She still is.
So were all the faces on the billboards
in the trolley cars

in the newspapers and books and moving picture houses.
They hurt my eyes.

Styles change; like dresses and houses and cars
and coca-cola bottles.
The coca-cola bottle was smaller
and cost a nickel.
One dime bought three pounds of onions.
Soap was not detergent.
Sapolio and Dutch Cleanser
had a monopoly all their own.
An ice-cream cone
a candy bar
even a loaf of bread
cost a nickel.

Milk was pasteurized
but not homogenized.
Newspapers cost three cents
a nickel or dime only on Sundays.
Magazines were monumental;
stories filled their pages with picture songs
and not just advertisements.
The pulps were full of mystery
and the dime novels flourished in kingdomville.
Streetcar trolleys were everywhere
with their hairline to the juice above them
and their feet firmly on the rails below them.
They had jim crow and seven cents fare.

Transportation by train was another thing.
The jim-crow cars were full of soot and cinders
the seats were hard
and the toilets were stinking holes

but white bankers rode at special rates
in special cars with kitchens and dining rooms
and beds and clean toilet facilities;
they had barbers and hairdressers
and coloured maids.
They chose the trains and not the planes.
Why did transportation change with integration?


## IV


Bobbed hair and short knee-high dresses and lipstick
and women smoking cigarettes in the street
were a form of liberation
only we called it emancipation.
Bathtub gin and raccoon coats with megaphones
at football games
were all part of our nineteen-twenties
with hayrides guaranteed to make a million or bust.
It burst.


Suddenly the grey flannel suits from Madison Avenue
appeared like the depression
from Coast to Coast.
Stores had bargain days.
Ford cars and Chevrolets
Studebakers, Packards, Willys Knights and Hudsons
Buicks and Rolls Royces
all had celluloid windows
and running boards.
Men wore high collars, spats and stetsons
Al Capone ruled Chicago

But by the time I got there
it was Dillinger.

A woman in a red dress fingered him
coming out of a picture show on the Near North Side.
Depression drunks
lay in gutters
sprawled on sidewalks
and men slept under newspapers in Grant Park
while looking for work.
There were soup kitchens and breadlines
and apples for sale on street corners.
Mr. Hoover told us
"Just around the corner
there's a rainbow in the sky."
Roosevelt's bloodless revolution
cleaned up the streets with the CCC
and the ERA and the WPA and the AAA.

Then we went to war
to resuscitate our dying economy
and make the world safe for prosperity.
Men died and died and died
so nickels could become quarters.
Now a dollar equals a dime.

The Sicilian brothers gave syndicated ideas to the world
and their Mafioso grew bold and strong:
Many different faces and many different races.
Stocking caps moved over their mouths.
Robbers and muggers mingled on street corners
and rose to high-rise apartment buildings
with multi-leveled offices and new neon lights;
but the streets never turned the lights back on;

they are still on war-time electricity.
While the G-Men became Federal
All the con-men went "legit"
Now they run our lives.
They speculate over our sepulchres and spit.

# MY TRUTH AND MY FLAME

I am a Black woman
and I hold my head up high,
for I rise with the masses of mankind. . . .
with the peoples of the earth;
I rise with the tides of revolution
against the systems of oppression
that hammer me down.

I am a Black woman
and my eyes speak history,
for I stand in the shadows of Time;
ever present from the beginnings,
ever ready for the struggle,
ever forceful with the waters
of perpetual changing time.

I am a Black woman
and my beauty is my power.
In my strength is the turning wind.
I am a flower, a fern, a tree.
I am the spirit in all living things
for I grow with my feet
in the rivers of destiny.

# CHICAGO

One day I saw Chicago river move
through milky dusk of twilight's lighted lamps.
I saw the avenues of moving lights
pour over Wacker Drive's slow blinking ramps.
I saw through fiery glow of foundry blasts
the river squatting low at dawn for steel.
Then in a filthy noon of stench-filled air
I saw the fouling river touch the slaughter pens.
I saw the freighted river moving on
through belching smoke of mill and boiler room
her river fingers washing in their hold
her lake and all its throngs of people fold
within their living and their daily toil
Her ancient meaning in their ageless tide.

# 1933

We were the breadlines.
Long queues waiting under Els for morning papers;
flop-house fellows, proud park-bench sleepers.

We were the stump speakers; the soap-box orators;
black bugs in Washington Park;
the hunger marchers, the strikers,
the fighters, the riot radicals.

We were the destitute, the cringers;
the unprepared unfortunates. . . .
Les Misérables . . . the poor.

We were the dreamers
the idlers, the slackers, the schemers
the stricken millions, underprivileged.

We were the boondogglers
wasting the money of the idle rich
and all the tax-payers' taxes.

# MONOLOGUE

I ain't never been scared of hard work.
I useta be a longshoreman on the levees
and sometimes when I was laid off
I useta break strikes, you know
what they calls a scab.
I dug ditches and I hauled ice and coal
and I followed the plow
many a day in the boiling hot sun
'cause when I got married
I worked a farm in the delta
and become a sharecropper;
but the white folks took all I made
and kept me heavy in they debt
and ain't nary one of my babies went to school
and my wife, she half-starved
and died with consumption.
Then this here depression come
and they say cotton ain't worth much
and they got a machine
what kin pick more in seben hours
than seben mens kin pick in t'ree months.
So I come up norf
and thought I'd git a job
'cause I'm a first class carpenter
but they wouldn't let me in the Union
and only Union mens gits work
so I had to git on relief
and they gimme a WPA job
making fifty-five dollars a month.
That wouldna been so bad

if I hadna caught cold
one day working in the rain on the job
and this here cough's been hanging on
ever since I left south.
You can tell I ain't never been lazy.
Hit just seems to me
Poah colored folks just naturally has a hard time
in a white folks world.

# ON YOUTH AND AGE II

**I**

I used to read the funny papers:
Maggie and Jiggs
Mutt and Jeff
and the Katzenjammer Kids.
Handlebar Harry isn't home any more,
and Rudolph the villain cries
"Curses! foiled again."
Now I don't like to read these violence strips,
strange capers of kooks and kinky ones.
Toots and Casper, and Barney Google
died a long time ago.
"Barney Google with his goo-goo-google eyes."
What's new? Peanuts.
Flash Gordon is an old guy from Space Land.
What's he doing here?
Where are all the funny faces?

Speakeasies and taverns, lounges, clubs, and corner saloons
are all the same.
They never went anywhere;
just played a changing game.
Where is the best place to find cocaine and pot
if not
in my classroom?
Maybe those pushers are outside on the playground
wearing clown faces?
Once, Mickey Finns were what you had to fear,

not someone dropping acid
in your tea or coffee
or an hypodermic needle.
Not any more.
Where did all our children go?
Overdosed on drugs.
Rotting in the pens.
Sleeping behind sofas.
Mama is drunk.
Daddy is money-mad, out chasing dollars and dames.
No more ice-cream cones.
They are all stoned.
They are sitting out the Act of Life
with empty faces, playing games.


**II**


This is my century:
Radio and picture-show;
Hot-rod, computer, video;
Ancient, rusty, slow auto:


*Ah-ooga, ooga, ooga*


Rumble seat and canvas coat.
"All you gals who smoke cigarettes
throw your butts in here."


Ante up the money.
Roll up the screens.

Clones and clowns and robots
Hear the lasers scream.

Soon there won't be any more.
We can't play Popeye and Olive Oyl forever.
Our century is about to expire.

Call the doctor; call the ambulance.
Get the fire department.
Put our feeble century in intensive care.
See if the old man can't last till tomorrow.
Everybody's getting burned up in this fire.


## III

Old shacks oughta be torn down:
Hundred-year-old rat traps;
Fire hazards and stinking johns
worse than outhouses
and old privies.
Roaches and rats are eating up the babies,
while the slummy, crummy basements
are still drawing the highest rent and killing death.

Once upon a time
black women cooked over fireplaces
baked biscuits in black iron stoves
trimmed neatly in ornamental nickel plate.
Coal, wood, and oil stoves
turned into gas and electricity.
Now when the sun is hot
heated to one hundred degrees fahrenheit
you can fry an egg

on the sidewalk
before any white man's front door.

I guess there's something called Energy
plaguing the world
with not enough to eat
and no clean water to drink
nothing but oil and coal and gas
from our fossilized world.
Now that there's nothing called electricity
in an electronic world full of space-time continuum
I guess there's something called Energy
making big problems for mankind
womankind and childrenkind too,
only I don't know why.
Didn't Galileo and Newton, Archimedes and Boyle,
Mr. "Con" Edison and Einstein know how?
Where did all the wizards go with our world?

# DISILLUSION
# FOR FLOWER CHILDREN
# OF LONG AGO

Brothers and Sisters, I will weep no more.
I will pray no more.
I will no longer prostrate myself
before gates of Power Structures.
I have lost my dream for you.
I have lost all hope for you.
I have lost my pure in heart.
I have lost our innocent.
They have put all my heroes of good will
through personality changes with drugs.
They have made my black panthers over
in behavior modification centers.
They have shackled our schizoid in Attica.
They have massacred the mass believers.
They have fed the children laughing, nerve, and mustard
        gas.
They have bombed the revolution in bed.
I stand here at Armageddon
and I see the whirlwinds rising:
Tornadoes in my southern land.
Volcanoes in your southern land.
I see dams of the damned
raging in white watercaps
floods of iniquity inundate us all.
I see lying preachers and whoremongers
dripping together with blood and gold.
Rapists and murderers repent;

forgiven they enter the kingdom;
but liars with honeyed lips
thieves walking through broad daylight
with moneybags they have taken
from old and sick and hungry;
merchants of the dream
selling and riding white horses;
Brothers and Sisters I hear these wailing ones
in this City of Dis.
Gnashing their teeth and moaning.
Brothers and Sisters,
I have lost my dream of life and love for you.
I have lost my hope for freedom, peace, and brotherhood for
    you.

# OLD AGE

I suffer now from stress;
the pain of living too long,
the clash of race and sex and class
against stark hunger of the world
for freedom, peace, and bread.
I suffer mainly from the stress and storm—
the way this planet moves
through power-drunken fools
who grovel in Uranian dust
for money in their greed
and in their evil lust.
They drive us all to hell,
polluting all the streams of life and love;
Forgetting how a flower forms—
a tree, a bird, a fawn,
a blue-grey world
without bright flaming orange-red
of sunlight setting on the sea;
beyond the blighted beige
of in-betweens,
immediate, and indeterminants.
So Black or Brown, Red, Yellow, White,
What difference does it make?
We all go down alike
Before their brutal strike
And Armageddon drives us down
To dig this human well
In dungeon hearts of hell.
I suffer now from stress.

# I HEAR A RUMBLING. . . .

I hear a rumbling underground.
I hear a rumbling. . . .
I hear my brothers underground
I hear a rumbling.

I hear an earthquake underground
I hear a rumbling.
I hear the red man underground
I hear a rumbling.

I hear the dead men from their graves
I hear them speaking
I hear the starving underground
I hear the rumbling

I hear Chicanos underground
I hear them grumbling
I hear the prisoners underground
I hear a rumbling

I hear a rumble and a grumble
I hear a rumbling
I hear the yellow and the brown men
I hear a rumbling

There are rockets in the air
There *is* a rumbling

There is lighting in the sky
There *is* a rumbling

I hear my children crying "Bread"
I hear my children crying "Peace"
I hear the farmers crying "Bread"
I hear the soldiers crying "Peace"

There is a rumbling. . . .

Guns and butter will not help.
We want Peace.
Dollars in the marketplace
We want Bread.

When the volcanoes erupt
We want Peace.
Bread and Peace are not enough;
Freedom too.

I hear a rumbling. . . .

They have boxed us in a coffin
Underground
They have chained us to a rock
Underground.

How long will their prices rise
to the skies?
How long must my children cry
to the skies?

How long will my people starve
Underground?

How long will the prisoners cry
Underground?

Christ is coming, so they say
In the skies.
Worlds will all be blown away
To the skies.

Will the earthquake underground
And the lighting in the skies
Peace and Bread and Freedom come
And the dead below arise?

There's a rumbling in the air
There's a lighting in the skies
There's a rumbling and a grumbling
And the walls of prisons breaking.

I hear rumbling underground
I hear rumbling.
Don't you hear the children crying?
Don't you hear the mothers weeping?

Blown to bits this craven crowd
Underground?
Blown to bits these plastic people
Underground?

Will you laugh or shout or cry?
Will you gloat and scream and die?

From the people everywhere
I have heard them here and there

Give us Freedom give us Peace
Give us Bread and Freedom, too
I hear rumbling underground
Peace and Bread and Freedom, too.

We will seize the power-mad
Everywhere
We will seize the guns and bread
Everywhere.

Give us Freedom, Give us Peace
I hear rumbling underground
Bread and Peace and Freedom too
I hear rumbling underground.

# DIES IRAE

The judgment of God is upon us.
The peace of the world stands at bay.
Our love hungers and yearns after the ways of Truth and
    Faith
and Mankind folded in the Divine swaddling clothes
as a suckling child
is lost.
Oh God of fire and holy tongues
where are your people today?
The Church of light has gone astray
whoring after Baal and other idol gods
The revelations of approaching hell and Armageddon
now torment us in waking dreams and sleep.
We seek Paradise
but we will be content
without the mystic ecstasy
to see thy Face and feel the healing touch of fire.
The footprints of Emmaus walk
even a distance from our troubled eyes
will take us to a well of constant springs;
will hush our fevered hearts
and quench desire.

# LOVE SONG FOR ALEX, 1979

My monkey-wrench man is my sweet patootie;
the lover of my life, my youth and age.
My heart belongs to him and to him only;
the children of my flesh are his and bear his rage
Now grown to years advancing through the dozens
the honeyed kiss, the lips of wine and fire
fade blissfully into the distant years of yonder
but all my days of Happiness and wonder
are cradled in his arms and eyes entire.
They carry us under the waters of the world
out past the starposts of a distant planet
And creeping through the seaweed of the ocean
they tangle us with ropes and yarn of memories
where we have been together, you and I.

# MEDGAR EVERS, 1925–1963

## Arlington Cemetery

So they laid him down in a beautiful place;
In a beautiful place to sleep and rest.
There his anguished life and our pulsing love
That beat in his heart and burned in his face,
They are quiet now, they are hushed and still,
But the world will forever mark this hill
Where they laid him down to sleep and rest
Where they laid him down in a beautiful place.

The birds overhead will build their nests;
In the twilight hours sing a serenade.
The grass will gradually creep into shade
Where this martyred man sleeps unafraid.
And he will have neighbors good and true
Who have given their lives for freedom, too.

# BIRMINGHAM, 1963

Out of my heart's long yearning
    from the fullness and futility
    of an overbearing patience and a suffering long
        waiting;
Out of the deepest long denial
    of sacrifice and slowly germinating complaint;
Through the streets of Birmingham
    the ghosts of bitter memories
    are waking and walking close with pain.
Hate is beseiged and beseeched in the streets
    of Birmingham. O my God, the naked pain
    in the streets and jails and alleys
    and the overlooking hills of Birmingham.

# JACKSON STATE, MAY 15, 1970

This is my black-eyed-susan school. These minds
    were touched by my black mind. And from riches
    of God's earth, sky, sea, and all inner recesses of
    hearts and spirits like ancient alchemists searching
    for secret veins, turning dross to gold, turning clay
    to consummately precious jewelry;
These are laughing eyes of many rainbowed faces who
    mill about streets, in rooms and halls of blackness
    turning lights from dim to bright; who search worlds'
    wide avenues adventuring to all corners of globes
    and turning into magicians—sleight of hand or
    legerdemain: marvelous men of medicine, theology,
    and letters, great operatic singers and teachers
    multimillionaire;
Not rich with gold but priceless truths of life and death, of
    giving self and sharing love for this is all there is. This
    is a thousand fold of beauty black and proud. This is
    my black-eyed-susan school.
Shotguns, high-powered rifles crackling in the night
    splattering glass and blood; screams cutting air with
    death and fright; ambulances and sirens wailing;
    streets covered with casings from their guns—highway
    patrolmen's guns. . . .
Death came and took our frozen young, our finest
    flowers, our black-eyed-susan boys and men, and
    wounded dozens more: women crouching in vain
    behind the broken window pane, lying along
    stairs, faces caricatured into spasms of
    despair.

Now all may see their faces in a marble monument, and walk this plaza where they died in vain; but we will not forget, for nothing is the same; never ever be the same since that blue-reddened night.

# THE TELLY BOOB-TUBE
# ON THE IDIOT BOX

Wake up Mister Morning.
Good Morning World.
Your new TODAY is here
with news for your no days
and no news for no today.
STOP.
TIME FOR COMMERCIAL MESSAGE:
Brother, can you spare a dime
for another cup of coffee
and another piece of pie
in the sky?
No poison. No sugar. No cream.
Just me, Myself, and Mine.
I am yours forever, for always, and for S-O-A-P
Here's suds in your eyes.
Sudsy, soapy, sugary, soapy, neat.
I am forever yours from Monday through Friday
But not on Saturday
That is my comic-strip morning
with all the bats and monsters out of hell
and gremlins out of outer space
and the horror-headed children who are sick.
"On the Seventh Day He rested from His labors."
So the garbage-hucksters deal out garbage
In His Name
for the price of a song that costs a few multi-million dollars:
send us a few multi-million dollars and we will send you this
     song
"Something Good is going to happen to you."

I just bet.
The psycho-sexual funny farm
Is On
from eight till late.
And after late they blow our minds
With everything from Sex and Nymphomania
to Arsonists with the oil-can and the fuse
to dynamite the world.
Why are they dilly-dallying with benzine
when all they want is benzedrine?
Do I wish to be entertained?
Or MUST I improve my Mind?
Sadists and Masochists are writing me
Off the Wall:
Programming me in prime time
for panic and paranoia.
Thank the nukes for nothing.
And all the game shows, beauty pageants and fashion
        fantasies
promising me something for nothing
Gambling my soul into hell
to get nothing, nothing, nothing. . . .
And then to pay the tax.

# AFRICA

THERE is something strange about Africa: Big letter "A"
There is something strangely large and wonderful;
something full of mystery; and something paradoxical
about her history.

ANCIENT mother of the world, the earth, of man;
custodian of the missing link, the dawning Age of the
Cyclops, cyclone, cockatoo, cricket, and cicada;

BEFORE monkeys were men and the bituminous, athracitic
earth turned coal to diamonds; before the carbon
change and acid test of timeless earth; before there was
a Was;

BEFORE the Garden of Eden and Allah near the Nile and
the Tigris and Euphrates in the land between the
rivers, before they harbored the Hebraic home of the
ancient Myth of Yahweh

BEFORE Isis and Osiris were born and the Sahara did
not exist, Africa with her mountains and plains and
rain forests was teeming Life. . . . hot and
wonderful life;

AND the races of men were cradled there. . . . black and
brown and yellow and red. The sun baked their
bread. . . . and the hot winds burned them to biscuit
brown, to mahogany red, to coal black blue earth from
whence they came.

LIFE did not begin in the cold white frozen northern
waste but in the hot black centers of earth where the

burning sands of desert lands and the hot volcanic
lanes of the mountain ranges cooled with the humidity
of rains.

AND the almond-eyed Orientals who slept beside the Yalu
and the Yangtze woke to call his black brother and the
red-brown Orientals who crossed the Bering strait on
land bridges and came to wildernesses of forest land
woke to remember their motherland Africa-Asia and
the pyramids they built were the same.

AND the Black Men in Africa rose up with spears in their
hands, made of bone, made of stone, made of the
Hittite Iron and they became hunters of Beasts. They
crossed plains and mountains and found antelope,

HUNTERS and shepherds grew in ancient lands where
mountains spoke; where churning volcanoes belched
smoke and rivers overflowing fertilized fields.

THERE is something strange about Africa; something
eternal, more than timeless and inexplicable: how a
giant sleeps; covering so much of all the earth; fertile
and rich and full of wondrous things; harboring life,
understanding all mysteries of death and time and
underworlds—how a giant sleeps.

O Mother Earth,
Dark Africa I come
to touch your sacred soil.
My ancient motherland,
Cradle of all our human lives,
Now tend these sacred fires.
Come, sacrifice your goat.

Raise altars from the myriad mountains' height
and heal our blinded sight.

How many wars and wounding battlelines have split your
    body-earth? Cutaneous broken veins have scarred your
    face? How many times have conquerors, colonizers,
    slavers, soldiers raped your bosom-earth?

THE green rain-forests shed your constant tears. The grey
    mountain rocks mourn your broken heart. And the
    deep desert sands take the winds into your vitals.

DEEP in your bowels lie the riches of the planet earth:
    Precious stones of rubies and diamonds, of gold and
    silver; minerals multiplicity, gurgling oil, Uranium
    galore, enough to fuel five centuries more electronic
    societies.

ALL fossilized energy rumbles in your belly. . . . gas and
    coal and copper mines leap up and burst in prodigality.

MAGIC speaks in all your medicinal, homeopathic herbs
    and sympathetic nerves. Throughout our centuries of
    man-made time your brooding spirit covers all.

YOUR sleeping giant slumbers fitfully and mumbles in his
    rest against the needling gnats and flies and insects
    leeching him.

Wake him, Mother Africa!
Wake your sleeping giant now.
Call all your sons to destiny.
The clarion call of yet another Age
now standing in the wings

demands your keening song
Awake and sing and call your deep enthralled
to destiny.
Awake, Arise, thrust up your dark, burned fist
against the dawning sky.
Awake I say, stand tall.
Our dear, dark, sweet, and wonderous Africa, stand tall!

# MONEY, HONEY, MONEY

Tell me, mama, what is it that makes the mare go round?
Money, honey, money.
What is it that makes that jingling sound?
Money, honey, money.
What is it that buys your pretty gown?
Money, honey, money.
What is it that helps to run this town?
Money, honey, money.
Tell me, mama, how do white folks keep the black folks
    down?
Money, honey, money.
And why do rich folks frown while poor folks clown?
Money, honey, money.
Even when you spin this pretty ditty:
Money, honey, money.
Everything boils down to this nitty-gritty
Money, honey, money.
I'll be glad when Money's out of style;
Money, honey, money.
Nothing but an ugly gory pile
Money, honey, money.
Ashes will be ashes and dust will go to dust
Money, honey, money.
Money can't go with you when your coffins rust
Money, honey, money.
Still the undertaker sings his daily song,
Money, honey, money.
And when the preacher says goodbye and gone,
Money is the thing you hear him say.
Money, honey, money all the way.

# ON POLICE BRUTALITY

I remember Memorial Day Massacre
Nineteen thirty-seven in Chicago.
And I was in the Capitol of D.C.
May of nineteen seventy-one
When they beat all those white heads
And put two thousand souls in jail.
I wasn't in South Commons Boston
Neither when Crispus Attucks died
Nor South Boston when the rednecks rioted.
But I remember Boston
Where I couldn't buy a hot pastrami sandwich
In a greasy joint.
I remember living there in fear
Much as some would feel in Mississippi.
I was neither in Watts, Los Angeles, California
In nineteen sixty-five
Nor Detroit in nineteen sixty-seven
And I remember all the fuss over LeRoi Jones
In Newark, New Jersey, too.
Now Santa Barbara, California is remembered
As a separate incident, a separate thing
From Kent State in Ohio
And Jackson State in Mississippi
And Orangeburg, South Carolina
And Texas Southern
But to me, they were all of one piece
Of the same old racist rag.
And all of these things are part
Of what I call Police Brutality.

# POWER TO THE PEOPLE

The invention of the wheel was long ago.
Horsepower preceded Galileo.
Even when the steamboats came along
Coal and steam and water were strong
Bearers of the people.
Trains and airplanes, washing machines
Dishwashers, dryers, and even hair-setters
Run by electricity.
And when the power fails
And they have a blackout in New Jersey
Darkness is not as bad
As a nuclear "accident"
The Rock of Gibraltar and the Rock of New York
Cannot withstand the power of the people.
Einstein saw a new universe
A new revolution of power and energy
And this is *his* century
Of atomic energy and spaceships to the moon
And bombs and warheads and nuclear accidents.
Power to the People?
You must be crazy.
Where do you think the CIA
And the FBI
The Mafia, and the Gnomes of Zurich will be?
Is Big Brother watching?
Yell, quick, if they are not looking,
POWER TO THE PEOPLE
Hush. . . . Listen to me whisper:
I didn't say a word.

# THEY HAVE PUT US ON HOLD

They have put us on HOLD.
They (the GI Government-Mafia-Fascist Dogs)
Have done a job on all Black People.
They have done a job of 'benign neglect'
Of Law and Order
Of Put down Black Insurrection in the streets
With the CIA
And the FBI
With the White Police
The National Guard
The Highway Patrol
And all the Armed Forces in the world.
They have turned the Rightist corner
To the Rich Conservative Ditch.
They monopolize the world.
They are the Prime Ministers
And Mister Bee is the President of the World.
They have killed all our Movements.
We can't walk anywhere.
We can't run anywhere.
We can't hide anywhere.
There is no place to go any more.
Peace and Bread and Justice are all in Jail with us.
They are holding Faith in irons
And they are building a gallows for Truth in the Yard.
There are no more Vigils for Peace.
(God bless the dead Quakers.)
There are no more marches for jobs.
(Jimmy Hoffa joined the Mafia and Mister Reuther is dead.)
The city lights are dimmed all over the world.

The streets are all deserted all over the world.
There is no more music from the Calliope.
The blackbirds are all jailbirds in the PEN
They have done a job on all Black People.
They have put us on HOLD.

# INFLATION BLUES

Inflation blues is what we got.
Poah Black folks must do without.
Can't buy no bread, can't buy no house.
Can't live no better than a louse.


We useta sing way back when
Depression was and come again:
"What's the matter with Uncle Sam?
He took away my sugar; now he's messing with my ham."


A piece of beef too high to buy;
Chicken ain't no better.
Fatback and fish too high to fry;
A quarter mails one letter.


It useta be when I was small
Ten dollars bought enough for y'all.
My daddy couldn't make one trip
From corner store to carry all.


This morning Lawd, I bought one bag
And "fifteen dollars" sez that ole hag.
I swallowed hard and bit my lip.
That sho was one expensive trip.


The gas too high to fill the tank
One year cost more than did the car

Bus fare so high I gotta walk
Cost more to live than foreign war.

You can't afford to live or die.
A baby cost too much to buy.
Hospital bed for just one day
Will scare your very death away.

I don't know what we coming to
The Gov'ment say they gonna do.
And all they do is raise the rent
And talk again how much they spent.

The wheat, the corn, and other grain
If it is dry, or if it rain
Must go across the world to feed
While we must pay and still must need.

Our city streets are full of crime
With robbers, muggers, raping blind.
Poah people can't afford to sleep.
Your house ain't safe, and you can't sweep

Your troubles underneath the rug
'Cause then that bad old carpet bug
Will rot you down, your house and all
Don't care which way you try to crawl.

Inflation blues is what we got.
Poah Black folks must do without.
We naked in the wind and blind
As jaybirds in moulting time.

# SOLACE

Now must I grieve and fret my little way
into death's darkness, ending all my day
in bitterness and pain, in striving and in stress;
go on unendingly again
to mock the sun with death
and mask all light with fear?
Oh no, I will not cease to lift my eyes
beyond those resurrecting hills;
a Fighter still, I will not cease to strive
and see beyond this thorny path a light.
I will not darken all my days
with bitterness and fear,
but lift my heart with faith and hope
and dream, as always, of a brighter place.

# FANFARE, CODA, AND FINALE

They are not for us any more: green fields where corn
    stands high; tasselled and bursting kernels glinting in
    sunlight, pits of clay where we went to play at dusk;
    blades of grass to chew idly and honeysuckle cups to
    sip; four o'clocks to string and morning glories to watch
    opening every afternoon and shutting tightly every
    morning; pretty pansies washing their faces in dew;
    these are lost flowers. Here underground we cannot see
    them any more. In the jails they will not let us look
    again.

Out of my lost laughter where my living once would flow,
    my song and my sadness are one. My joy and pain are
    bound one on one. . . . In the laughing rhythms of my
    singing tears are part of my living and my tears rain
    through my laughing eyes bitter, bitter, bitter through
    and through.

I buy bread of bitterness everyday in the markets of the
    world. Peace and plenty are never my share; every day I
    go hungry. Everyday I walk in fear, and no one seems
    to care.

Black kings on their thrones who lived a thousand years ago
    are part of me now. Even they must share my bitter
    bread. When I beg, it is bitter bread they toss to me to
    eat. When I work, it is bitter bread I win from my toil.
    Even the mealy ash cake I bake in my humble hut is
    borrowed bread, is bitter, borrowed bread.

Grant me one song to sing, America, out of my hurt and
    bruised dignity; let notes confused and bursting in my

throat find melody. Reprieve the doom descending on my life. Remake the music stifling in my throat. Before my song is lost resound the tune and hear my voice.

Out of my struggle I have sung my song; found hymn and flower in field and fort and dungeon cell. Yet now I have constriction in my heart where song is born. Such bitterness is eating at my vocal chords the bells within me, hushed, refuse to ring. Oh lift this weight of brick and stone against my neck, and let me sing.

# FARISH STREET

# THE AFRICAN VILLAGE

In our beginnings our Blackness was not thought so
    beautiful
but out of bitterness we wrought an ancient past
here in this separate place
and made our village here.
We brought our gifts to altars of your lives
with singing, dancing, giving,
and moved stumbling stones into the market place.

Dark faces of our living generations
hear voices of our loving dead go echoing
down corridors of centuries.
For those who suffered, bled and died
Let this be monument:
the passing throngs parade before our eyes again.
Our children playing here
our neighbors passing by;
the daily swift encounters hear
and whispering in alleys,
dark corners of our lives
resuscitate.

In this short street a class of Africans create
A jungle world, a desert and a plain,
A mountain road, rain forests, and valleys
green and sweet.
We touch the earth and sky and flowers bloom
around our quivering feet.
Sunshine and rain
beat on these stones and bricks,

and wooden windowpanes.
Green grass grows scantily
and skirts the blackened pools on
muddy streets.
Thundershowers, snow, and sunlight
stream through an open doorway—
Syrian butcher in his bloody apron;
Green grocer with his sidewalk wares,
And hucksters riding wagons down this road
With a cry
for everyone to come and buy.
This is a place of yesteryears,
forgotten street of dreams.
The stardust shines
into the crevices of dingy lives
and gleams across our listlessness.
Oh! hear the song
Go whistling down the empty years
and let the afterglow
of all my hoped tomorrows
Fall on my lonely shadow.

I'll hawk your dreams,
your broken stars of glass
I'll paint your visions
on a rainbow road
that shines across dark starry skies.

# A PATCHWORK QUILT

This street is like my grandma's patchwork quilt
Kaleidoscope, appliqued with multicolored
threads of embroidery.
A golden sun, blue skies, carpeted with the greenness
the yellow, the red, the white, the black, the brown, and
the checkered.
Bright gingham, fine silk and satin and linen cloth
patterned patches on the faces of these people
the Chinese laundryman
Black cobbler
Greek grocer
And down the street there used to be
A livery stable with a brown Indian man.
Now there's a taxi stand.
Once streetcars passed along the side
Up Capitol
to where black slaves built the Capitol
the mansion for the governor
and over there, the city hall.
They made these bricks and laid them too
Not knowing some day they would meet
As Black and Tan in 1868.
This patchwork quilt is stitched with blood and tears
This street is paved with martyred Black men's flesh and
        bones.

# THE CRYSTAL PALACE

The Crystal Palace used to be
a place of elegance
Where "bourgie" black folks came to shoot
a game of pool
And dine in the small cafe
across the way.
The dance hall music rocked the night
and sang sweet melodies:
"Big fat mama with the meat shaking on her bones"
"Boogie woogie mama
Please come back home"
"I miss you loving papa
but I can't live on love alone"
The Crystal Palace
Used to be
most elegant.

# THE HOUSE OF PRAYER

Two undertaking parlors on this street
close to the House of God
have witnessed all the shame of Farish
    Street.
In another life Sister Sadie Lou
was like that gal from Madame's Fancy
    House
Bawdy Belle with her tight spanky-baby
    dress
her cigarette
her blood-red pasted lips on a clown's
    face
high heeled shoes
and lacquered hair
and her shoulder bag
swinging down her hips
full of tricks.
Hey gal, what you selling
On Farish Street?
And she laughs a hollow joyless sound
Oh, you know you know, I know you
    know—
*Mary Mack, dressed in black*
*Silver buttons*
*All down her back.*
*I like sugar*
*I like tea*
*I love pretty girls*
*And they love me.*
*Ask my mama*

*for fifteen cents*
*to see the elephant*
*jump the fence*
*jump so high*
*Touched the sky*
*Didn't come back*
*Till the fourth of July.*

# SMALL BLACK WORLD

Fly away birdies, fly away home.
Pigeons roosting
Gray as the dawning
Gray as the winter morning
Fly away birdies, fly away.
All our history is here
All our yearning, dreaming, hoping, loving, dying
All our lives are buried here
See that old blind man
He is led by a child
And his tin cup in his hand
jingles coins like bells of the Calliope
A monkey on a string dances to the tune
of an organ-grinder
Shrill paddy wagon rushing crowds
Drunken, stoned, and crazy
slashing stabbing knives and razors cutting throats
sirens screaming
lookers-on shrieking
scattering and disappearing
flooding bloody Farish Street.
While the shuffling feet of ghosts who are prisoners in the
    night
pass into yesterday.
On the corner gray stone rises.
A black man's name is on the building:
Federal building on his land
Like the Reservoir on black land
Like the river roads on black land.
I have walked these streets all over the world

*Farish Street*    205

Black streets, Farish Streets
where all the black people all over the world
have set up their shops
in the markets of the world
where we sell our souls daily to every passerby
and our children come to play in emptiness
and softly night falls suddenly.

# BLACK MAGIC

There's a magic man on Farish Street
Root doctor, hoodoo man
Sells charms and potions
"Cross the river for liquor
And bring your own bottle to the party."
They are playing checkers in the twilight
Before the barber shop,
Before the beauty parlor
Before the drug store where the man sells
       magic:
Love charms and potions and good luck
       pieces,
powders, and odors, and aphrodisiacs
High John the Conqueror and
Sampson Snake Root;
Across from the YW and the YMCA
Where the saints go marching in
Where the street dead-ends
And the cemetery begins
The other side of the tracks
There's a man selling lucky charms
And he sells bargains too
Choose between God and the devil
Choose between flesh and the spirit
Choose between sacred and the profane
But remember, when you sell your soul to the
       devil
Prepare to live in hell!
Black man you know well
Lie down with dogs and get up with fleas

*There's a man going round taking names*
*Lawd knows they scandalizing my name*
*I want Jesus to make up my dying bed*
when they carry my coffin down Farish Street
pigeon-toed and wrinkled nosed
sidling up to fate.

# THE LABYRINTH OF LIFE

I have come through the maze and the mystery of living
to this miraculous place of meaning
finding all things less than vanity
all values overlaid and blessed with truth and love and peace
having a small child's hand to touch
a kiss to give across a wide abyss
and knowing magic of reconciliation and hope;
To a place blessed with smiling
Shining beyond the brightness of noonday
and I lift my voice above a rising wind
to say I care
because I now declare
this place called Farish Street in sacred memory
to be one slice of life
one wheel of fortune a-turning in the wind
and as I go
a traveller through this labyrinth
I taste the bitter-sweet waters of Mara
and I look to the glory of the morning of all life.
AMEN. I say AMEN.